Handbook on Differentiated Instruction

for Middle and High Schools

Sheryn Spencer Northey

EYE ON EDUCATION
6 DEPOT WAY WEST, SUITE 106
LARCHMONT, NY 10538
(914) 833–0551
(914) 833–0761 fax
www.eyeoneducation.com

Library of Congress Cataloging-in-Publication Data

Northey, Sheryn.
Handbook on \ differentiated instruction for middle and high schools / Sheryn Northey.
       p. cm.
Includes bibliographical references.
ISBN 1-930556-93-4
   1. Individualized instruction. 2. Mixed ability grouping in education. 3. Cognitive styles in children. 4. Middle school teaching. 5. High school teaching. I. Title.
   LB1031.N65 2005
   373.13'94--dc22

                                                     2004021281

   10 9 8 7 6 5 4 3 2 1

Editorial and production services provided by
Richard H. Adin Freelance Editorial Services
52 Oakwood Blvd., Poughkeepsie, NY 12603-4112
(914-471-3566)

Meet the Author

Sheryn Northey is presently the Academic Facilitator (lead teacher) at Northwest School of the Arts in Charlotte, North Carolina. Her many accomplishments include "Teacher of the Year" in two schools, National Board Certification (1997), and Founding Fellow for the Teacher's Network Leadership Institute. She came to teaching after working for several years as a psychotherapist and consultant. She is a licensed mentor and a licensed teacher of Academically and Intellectually Gifted students. She also is a member of the Board of Trustees for the North Carolina Center for the Advancement of Teaching and has worked on several local, state, regional, and national projects to promote quality teaching. She works with ArtsTeach, an organization whose vision is to integrate arts and academics, and she provides professional development classes for the Charlotte-Mecklenburg School District on a variety of topics.

TABLE OF CONTENTS

Introduction

What Is Differentiation?

Although most teachers have some idea what the term differentiation of instruction means, I will define it here to ensure that novice and veteran teachers are thinking about this concept the way I have conceptualized it. Differentiation of instruction means tailoring instruction to meet the various needs of students. I agree with Carol Ann Tomlinson (Tomlinson, 1995) who says that we should differentiate instruction based on a student's readiness to learn a concept or skill, their interest in learning that concept or skill (or using their interests as a way to motivate them to learn a skill or concept), and their style of learning that concept or skill. We use strategies that adjust the content we teach, the process in which we teach it, and the products we ask students to give us so that we can determine their achievement in learning a concept or skill.

Why Differentiate?

Although not easy, there are at least two good reasons to learn how to implement differentiation in secondary school. The most important is that it is the only fair way to teach, and somewhat less important, but definitely a reality, is that most school districts and parents insist on it.

Just because differentiation is fair and required doesn't mean most secondary teachers feel they can be successful at it. For instance, how can one teacher actually *know* as many as 150 or more students, much less be able to align instruction to meet their individual needs? Differentiation of instruction is easy for superintendents, parents, and principals to require, but hard for teachers to do, especially new teachers.

The purpose of this book is to help teachers, novice to master teachers, learn that differentiation is possible and rewarding. All you need is some planning time to:

- Get to know your students.
- Gather resources.
- Determine the best differentiation process to accomplish your goals.
- Plan strategies for determining acceptable evidence of learning, and
- Put all your work into units and daily lesson plans.

How to Use This Book

This book is differentiated to meet the needs of busy teachers who do not have the time or interest in wading through paragraphs of theory to get to the "how to do it" phase. I suggest you read through each step quickly to get the basic ideas, and then actually *take* each step and try the suggestions with which you are most comfortable.

This book is formatted to enable you to find information quickly and easily. Resources and models are provided for you to use. At times you are directed to a resource that you may need to access yourself. The suggestions herein are a blend of real life teaching experience from my work as a National Board Certified classroom English/Language Arts teacher, an Academic Facilitator (lead teacher for academic subjects) in a grades 6–12 arts magnet school, and as a professional developer for my district.

I hope you will be able to implement many of these suggestions because if you do not learn to differentiate instruction, your students will suffer. If you had several children to feed each day, you would not feed only certain ones and let the others starve. If you were providing care to sick children, you would not just treat certain children and let the others die. As a teacher, you can no longer teach only the students who respond to your current teaching methods and let the others fall behind or drop out of the education process altogether.

1

Getting to Know Your Students

Step 1—Know Your *Own* Learning Styles

Before you begin to learn about your students, you should first know *yourself*, your learning preferences and abilities. Hopefully, most of us who teach are fairly well-rounded and can address most students' needs; however, I would challenge you to look at the role your own learning preferences play in how you plan instruction, especially if you have a student or students who are not learning well in your class. You may determine that your learning preferences are in conflict with your student's preferences.

For instance, I know that my "mind style" is "abstract sequential." That means that I am hard working, intellectually organized, see the big picture, and enjoy exploring multiple perspectives (among many other traits). If I am teaching students who tend to prefer less traditional classrooms, who have issues with authority, and who become bored with classes that are too abstract and not experiential, I will need to stretch both cognitively and emotionally. I have to be respectful of our differences and find ways to adjust my values and my teaching if I want to help those students succeed in my class.

The first suggestion is that you find out about *yourself* (if you don't already know). The work of Dr. Anthony Gregorc is especially impressive. He has developed the concept of "Mind Styles." "Mind Styles" include these categories: "Concrete Sequential," "Concrete Random," "Abstract Sequential," and "Abstract Random." You can go on line at http://www.gregorc.com to get information about the "Style Delineator." Dr. Gregorc has not normed this test for children or young people; therefore, teachers should not test students with it. Teachers, however, could use this measurement tool in order to know their own "Mind Styles" so that they might be more effective with various learners.

Here are several other inventories that teachers could use to assess their learning styles. Anyone can take a test called "The Learning Type Measure" (LTM) online at http://64.226.183.123/ltm-purchase.htm (cost is $8.00) to find

1

out which kind of learner they are. The four types of learners according to this model are as follows:

- ♦ Type 1—Innovative Learner,
- ♦ Type 2—Analytic Learner,
- ♦ Type 3—Common Sense Learner, and
- ♦ Type 4—Dynamic Learner.

Other inventories that assess learning styles and personality are as follows:

- ♦ The *Index of Learning Styles Questionnaire* (Solomon and Felder, 1993) online at http://engr.ncsu.edu/learningstyls/ilsweb.html to take this free test.
- ♦ The Myers-Briggs Type Indicator (MBTI) (Myers, McCaulley, 1985) online at http://www. humanmetrics.com/cgi-win/JTypes2.asp
- ♦ The Kiersey Temperament Sorter II (Kiersey, 1998) online source is http://www. advsorteam.com

Remember, some inventories you fine online may be for adults only and may not necessarily be highly scientific; therefore, use good judgment when using them and responding to what you find.

Another suggestion is that you learn about yourself as you explore how you will learn about your students. If you plan to ask students to take an inventory, you should have already taken it yourself to evaluate whether the results seem valid.

Strive to be a role model to your students by knowing your learning preferences and stretching yourself to become a well-rounded and successful learner in many environments and for many tasks. After all, most teachers understand that the key to success in most school communities is flexibility!

Step 2—Believe You Can Know All of Your Students

Can one teacher know the learning preferences, interests, and abilities of, at times, over 150 students? Not easily—many teachers throw up their hands and say, "I can't!" But there are at least two strategies that can make it possible for you to plan differentiation for all of your students.

Strategy 1—Encourage Self-Discovery

Constantly remind your students that they should find out about themselves as learners, so that they may become interested in and advocates for their own education. Help them understand that they should become responsible experts on how they learn best. Give them many opportunities to explore their learning styles and abilities.

This strategy should begin as early as possible. If elementary grade teachers have not helped students understand they are responsible for learning, you must teach them at whatever grade level you have them.

Strategy 2—Documentation

Document the learning needs of every student (use the "Differentiation Data Sheet" provided at the end of the chapter). Keep at least one sheet of information on each of your students. Let your students know that you are truly interested in how they learn best. Assure them that you will collaborate with them to provide the best learning environment within your sphere of influence to help them meet their needs.

Share your learning preferences with students and help them become your partner in their education. Assure them that you are not "the enemy," but that you want to help them succeed in school.

Step 3—Obtain Reading Information

An essential early step is to determine how well each student reads your major source of content information. For many teachers, this will be the district assigned student textbook. Any students who have difficulty accessing information through your major source of content information would most likely have a hard time succeeding in your class.

Strategy 1—Assessing the Readability of Your Major Text

- ◆ Choose a typical page in your major text.
- ◆ Read it to yourself to establish the speed at which an accomplished reader would read it.
- ◆ Write at least five basic comprehension questions.
  - • Do not write questions that are tricky or that ask students to recall minute details.
  - • Ask questions that require students to have a basic idea of what they have just read. (Hint: After you read that page, think about what *you* remember. You may be surprised.)
- ◆ During class, tell students that you are going to conduct an experiment. Tell them you are going to find out how readable their text-

book is. Enlist their cooperation and interest in making this experiment work for you and for them.

♦ Ask students to turn to that same page in their books.

♦ Ask them to take out a sheet of paper and write their names and title of the text at the top of the paper.

♦ Tell them that they are going to help you find out how well they read the text. Tell them they will be timing themselves, and then answering some comprehension questions.

♦ Make sure the clock has a second hand.

♦ Make sure everyone understands how the clock works and how to record the time in minutes and seconds.

♦ Tell them that when they finish reading the page, they should look up at the time and record it on the sheet of paper.

♦ Start everyone at the same time. Record the start time on the board.

♦ After everyone has read, give everyone the five-question comprehension quiz. (Check to make sure everyone has recorded a stop time.)

♦ Finally, ask students to read the page again to make a list of any words for which they were not sure the meaning.

♦ Ask students to turn in that paper.

Assessment

Students who meet the following criteria *do not* have access to information through your text:

♦ Read significantly slower than you.

♦ Made more than two errors on comprehension test.

♦ Listed five or more words they did not know.

Students who meet the following criteria, *do* have access to information through your text:

♦ Read slightly slower than you.

♦ Made no more than one or two errors on the comprehension test.

♦ Listed no more than five words they did not know.

Students who meet the following criteria, *need enrichment materials* to supplement the text:

♦ Read as fast or faster than you.

♦ Made no errors on comprehension text.

♦ Listed no words they did not know.

I created this method, which I have used in several classes. It gives me a quick assessment of student's reading abilities in their textbooks (Northey, 2004).

Strategy 2—Use Other Readability Assessments

Fry's Readability Graph

Find out the Lexile Level of your text by using this formula from Fry's Readability Graph: Clarifications, Validity, and Extensions to Level 17 (Edward B. Fry, 1977).

Fry's Readability Graph

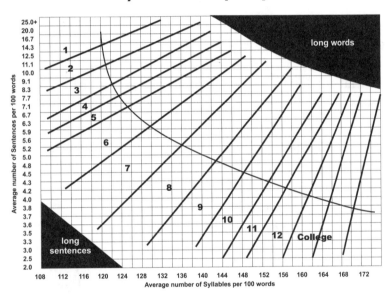

Expanded Directions for Working Readability Graph

1. Randomly select 3 sample passages and count out exactly 100 words each, beginning with the beginning of a sentence. Do count proper nouns, initializations, and numerals.

2. Count the number of sentences in the hundred words, estimating length of the fraction of the last sentence to the nearest one-tenth.

3. Count the total number of syllables in the 100-word passage. If you don't have a hand counter available, an easy way is to simply put a mark above every syllable over one in each word, and then when you get to the end of the passage, count the number of marks and add 100. small calculators can also be used as counters by pushing numeral 1, then push the + sign for each word or syllable when counting.

4. Enter on the graph the average sentence length and average number of syllables; plot dot where the two lines intersect. The area where the dot is plotted will give you the approximate grade level.

5. If a great deal of variability is found in the syllable count or sentence count, putting more samples into the average is desirable.

6. A word is defined as a group of symbols with a space on either side; thus, Joe, IRA, 1945, and & are each one word.

7. A syllable is defined as a phonetic syllable. Generally, there are as many syllables as vowel sounds. For example, *stopped* is one syllable and *wanted* is two syllables. When counting syllables for numerals and initializations, count one syllable for each symbol. For example, 1945 is four syllables, IRA is three syllables, and & is one syllable.

Lexiled Test

Another suggestion is to determine if your students have taken a standardized reading test that has been "Lexiled." Note if your student's reading level is within range of that Lexile. If the student's reading level is below the level for your text then that student does not have access to content information through your text. If their Lexile level exceeds that of your text, you need to supplement the text.

Author's note: The Lexile level of many novels may be found by going to this Web site: www.lexile.com

Cloze Test

Finally, another way to determine readability is to make a "Cloze Test" from your textbook. You can take a page out of your textbook, type it, and leave out every tenth word. If students are able to successfully insert words that keep the original meaning of the text, then the text is readable for them. If they have little or no idea which words can be inserted to make meaningful sentences, then the text is too difficult.

Strategy 3—Use Standardized Test Assessments of Student Reading Levels

Using standardized reading test scores will help you determine if students have access to content information through your text.

Use these guidelines:

♦ If students scored well-below grade level or below grade level, they will not have access to content information through your text. Most texts are leveled the same way standardized tests are, so that students' scores will reflect their ability to read on-grade-level materials.

- If they score at grade level, they will have access to information through your text, although you may need to scaffold some information in most technical areas.
- Students who score well above grade level on reading tests, should have access to enrichment materials to supplement your text.

Most reading researchers agree that struggling readers need to build their reading strengths by reading materials on their current grade level, and that these readers cannot build reading skills on texts that are above their reading level. There is an implied expectation that teachers do not expect all students to access information through a text, and that the teacher must "scaffold" (provide temporary support) the information for below grade level readers. Although scaffolding (which will be detailed later) is an excellent way to help struggling readers improve, too much scaffolding can handicap them because it teaches them that they do not need to access content information through reading because the teacher will tell them what they need to know.

It is interesting that many districts do not provide leveled texts for teachers to use with students who are reading below grade level. Many textbooks have aligned texts that match content, but are written two or three levels below grade level. In some cases, these materials are only available to students who are certified learning disabled.

Step 4—What Are Your Students' Learning Styles or Preferences?

There is a wealth of information (a lot of it is on the Internet, and, therefore, easily accessible) about determining a person's learning style or preference; therefore, you have several choices of inventories, checklists, and questionnaires to help you and your students determine how you learn best. Five of them are presented here for you. You can decide which of these fit your own philosophy of learning:

Strategy 1—Left-Brain/Right-Brain?

Although neuroscience does not support this concept, students and educators enjoy rating themselves according to brain dominance.

Find out from which side of the brain you function most, and then find out the same for each student. If you are mostly left-brained and the majority of your students are mostly right-brained, you may run into some problems understanding each other. See the "Brain Scan" adapted from Dr. Ron Rubenzer to help you determine your brain side preference.

Brain Scan

Check all statements that apply to you. Add up the checks on both sides. The side with the most checks is your dominant side. Work to use both sides of your brain.

Name: _____ Date: _____

Left Brain	*Right Brain*
___ Analytical (breaks things down)	___ Analogical (makes connections)
___ Ask factual questions (who, what, where, why)	___ Ask speculative questions (what if, why not)
___ Astronomy buff	___ Astrology fan
___ By the clock (e.g., lunch is always at noon)	___ Timeless (lunch is "whenever" you are hungry
___ Doer	___ Dreamer
___ Enjoy complicated	___ Keep it simple
___ Early bird	___ Night owl
___ Exactness and precision desired	___ Exaggerate at times
___ Focused, narrow	___ Nebulous, diffuse
___ Intellectual	___ Artistic
___ Interested in science fact	___ Interested in science fiction
___ Loathes surprises	___ Loves surprises
___ Logical	___ Intuitive
___ Makes order out of chaos	___ Makes chaos out of order
___ Motivated by external rewards	___ Motivated by satisfaction
___ Opinionated	___ Open-minded
___ Planned	___ Directionless
___ Prefer clarity	___ Prefer vagueness
___ Prefer correct answer	___ Seek alternative responses
___ Rule maker	___ Rule breaker/bender
___ Serious	___ Jokster
___ Structured, forced	___ Unstructured, free
___ Task oriented	___ Idea oriented
___ Test ideas	___ Make ideas
___ Uptight	___ Uninhibited
___ Verbal	___ Visual
_____ LB Column total	_____ RB Column total

From Rubenzer, R. (2003, February). How the Best Handle Stress. Warren Publishing (warrenpublish@aol.com, 1-704-892-2940).

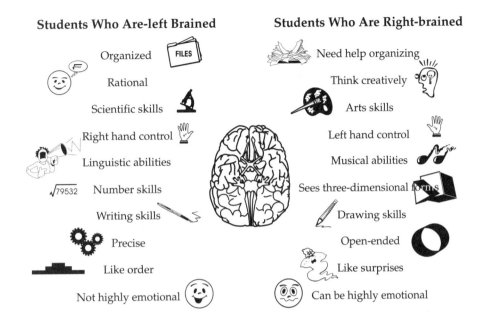

Students Who Are-left Brained

Organized

Rational

Scientific skills

Right hand control

Linguistic abilities

Number skills

Writing skills

Precise

Like order

Not highly emotional

Students Who Are Right-brained

Need help organizing

Think creatively

Arts skills

Left hand control

Musical abilities

Sees three-dimensional forms

Drawing skills

Open-ended

Like surprises

Can be highly emotional

Learning Strategies

Strategies That Left-Brained Students Might Use	*Strategies That Right-Brained Students Might Use*
Flash cards	Pictures or picturing information
Outlines	Graphic organizers
Memorizing information	Mnemonic songs or actions
Getting up early to study	Staying up late to study
Scheduling exact study times	Studying whenever it feels right
Breaking ideas down into chunks of information	Connecting ideas with feelings and past experiences
Taking notes on the facts	Getting a sense of the big ideas or concepts
Getting a friend to quiz them	Think time
Choosing learning tasks that have right answers	Choosing learning tasks that have many ways of showing mastery

Strategy 2—Visual, Auditory, or Kinesthetic/Haptic Learners?

Know your students' learning style preferences. A learning style is a preference for the method by which an individual learns something and how that individaul remembers what has been learned. There are three basic modes according to most experts: visual, auditory, and kinesthetic/haptic. Visual learners learn best through their sense of sight. Auditory learners learn best through hearing. Kinesthetic/haptic learners learn by doing or experiencing, which includes kinesthetic, olfactory, and tactile learning. The way students receive information is of foremost importance in designing instruction to meet their needs. Visual and auditory learners usually do all right in most classrooms; unfortunately, however, kinesthetic/haptic learners have fewer opportunities to utilize their learning preference.

There is a free Learning Styles Inventory by Dr. Pat Wyman at www.howtolearn.com. You and your students can get immediate feedback that includes what percentage you use of each of the three learning styles.

Strategies Used by		
Visual Learners	*Auditory Learners*	*Kinesthetic/Haptic Learners*
Read the information	Listen to someone speak the information	Do an activity or lab to experience the information
See a film that explains information	Listen to the information on tape	Role play the information
Memorize by using flash cards	Memorize by repeating information to self or partner	Memorize by remembering and experiencing the information
Find a quiet place to study	Find a place to study out loud	Find a place to move around while studying
Doodle while learning	Have music on while learning	Get a chance to try different ideas while learning
See pictures when reading	Hear the writer's words when reading	Need lots of breaks when reading
Writing information helps make it memorable	Discussing information helps make it memorable	Experiencing information helps make it memorable

It is important to know your preferred method of obtaining information, so that you can make sure you address the needs of your students who do not share your preference. Find colleagues or even students who have preferences different from yours. Ask them to look at your lesson plans and let you know if you are including methods of learning that allow them to access information from your teaching. There are teaching strategies that I will present later in the book that address planning lessons that address these learning preferences.

Dr. Lynn O'Brien (1990) conceptualized "Learning Channel Preferences" as a way to help students improve their ability to learn. If you go to her Web site, www.way2go.com, you can order a copy of her test to determine learning preferences. Here is an adapted copy of a survey.

To determine if your students are auditory, visual, or kinesthetic/haptic learners, have them take the "Learning Channel Preference" checklist as follows:

Learning Channel Preference

Name:_____   Date:_____

Read each sentence carefully and consider whether or not it applies to you.

3	2	1	0
Often Applies	*Sometimes Applies*	*Almost Never Applies*	*Never Applies*

Add up the numbers and the channel with the highest score is your learning channel preference.

A   *Channel* _____

____   1.   When I read, I listen to the word in my head or read aloud.

____   2.   To memorize something, it helps me to say what I am trying to learn over and over to myself.

____   3.   I need to talk about things to understand them.

____   4.   I don't need to take notes in class.

____   5.   I remember what people have said, better than what they were wearing.

____   6.   I like to record things to listen to on tape.

____   7.   I'd rather hear a lecture on something rather than have to read about it.

____   8.   I can easily follow a speaker even when I am not watching the speaker talk.

____   9.   I talk to myself when I'm solving a problem or writing.

____   10. I prefer to have someone tell me how to do something rather than to read the directions myself.

____   **A   Total**

B   *Channel* _____

____ 1. I don't like to read or listen to directions; I'd rather just start doing.

____ 2. I learn best when I am shown how to do something and then have the opportunity to do it.

____ 3. I can study better when music is playing.

____ 4. I solve problems more often through trial-and-error, rather than using a step-by-step approach.

____ 5. My desk and/or locker look disorganized.

____ 6. I need frequent breaks while studying.

____ 7. I take notes but never go back to read them.

____ 8. I do not become easily lost, even in strange surroundings.

____ 9. I think better when I have the freedom to move around; I have a hard time studying at a desk.

____ 10. When I can't think of a specific word, I'll use my hands a lot and call something a "thing-a-ma-jig."

____ **B** **Total**

C   *Channel* _____

____ 1. I enjoy doodling and even my notes have lots of pictures, arrows, and other marks on them.

____ 2. I remember something better if I write it down.

____ 3. When I am trying to remember a telephone number, or something new, it helps me to picture it in my head.

____ 4. When I am taking a test, I can "see" the textbook page and the correct answer on it.

____ 5. Unless I write down directions, I am likely to get lost or arrive late.

____ 6. It helps me to look at the person speaking. It keeps me focused.

____ 7. I can clearly picture things in my head.

____ 8. It's hard for me to understand what a person is saying when there is background noise.

____ 9. It's difficult for me to understand a joke when I hear it.

____ 10. It's easier for me to get work done in a quiet place.

____ **C** **Total**

Key: Channel A—Auditory Learner, Channel B—Kinesthetic Learner, Channel C—Visual Learner

(O'Brien, 1990)

Strategy 3—The 4Mat System

The 4Mat System developed by Bernice McCarthy (1981) provides a specific model for assessing and addressing varied learning styles. It is based on work by Gregorc and Butler (1984) and Kolb (1984).

The 4Mat System suggests that most people have a dominant learning style based on three major tendencies:

- right-brained or left-brained tendencies,
- abstract and concrete tendencies,
- active and reflective tendencies.

McCarthy suggests that teachers should plan units of study that do the following:

- address all of these tendencies, so that students will be stretched to develop a cognitive flexibility,
- support and nurture all learning preferences,
- make sure students understand themselves as learners, and
- help students appreciate learning differences.

By doing these four things, teachers facilitate the possibility that students will be more successful as they learn a wide variety of concepts and skills. The 4Mat System provides a graphic organizer that helps teachers plan units of study that address the four learning styles. Each style has a dominant question, strengths, and choices among eight modes based on right brain and left brain preferences: (1) Connecting, (2) Examining, (3) Imaging, (4) Defining, (5) Trying, (6) Extending, (7) Refining, and (8) Integrating. Each mode is sequenced in the specified steps as follows:

Abstract

(Active Side)	(Reflective Side)
Quadrant 4 Dynamic Learner Dominant Question: If? Strengths: Creating, risking, adapting, modifying Modes: Left brain-refining (Step 7) Right brain—integrating (Step 8)	**Quadrant 1** Imaginative Learner Dominant Question: Why? Strengths: Brainstorming, interacting, listening, speaking Modes: Right brain-connect (Step 1) Left brain—examine (Step 2)
Quadrant 3 Common Sense Learner Dominant Question: How? Strengths: Experimenting , manipulating, improving, tinkering Modes: Left brain—try (Step 5) Right brain—extend (Step 6)	**Quadrant 2** Analytic Learner Dominant Question: What? Strengths: Analyzing, classifying, observing, theorizing Modes: Right brain—image (Step 3) Left brain—define (Step 4)

Concrete

For more information, go to www.aboutlearning.com

Strategy 4—The Four Learning Styles

Silver, Strong, and Perini (2000) base their ideas of learning styles on the work of Carl Jung (1933) who conceptualized four dimensions of personality: thinking, sensing, feeling, and intuition. They also used the work of Isabel Myers (1985) who adapted Jung's ideas to develop the famous Myers-Briggs Type Indicator (MBTI). They use the quadrant idea, similar to 4Mat, with a few differences. Here is their "Four Learning Styles" indicator:

Sensing (**S**)

	Sensing/Thinking (ST) Mastery Style	Sensing/Feeling (ST) Interpersonal Style	
Thinking (**T**)	Intuitive/Thinking (NT) Understanding Style	Intuitive/Feeling (NF) Self-Expressive Style	Feeling (**F**)

Intuition (**N**)

Note: "N" is used for intuition because in Jung's theory, "I" was used for *Introversion*.

You and your students could do the self-assessments included in this book, to determine your style, or you can look at behaviors for each style and think about which one fits you and your individual students best.

Each of the four learning styles is explained briefly in the following organizer (adapted from Silver, Strong, and Perini, 2000, p. 28):

Mastery Style	*Interpersonal Style*
Learns best by: ♦ Seeing concrete evidence ♦ Practicing ♦ Knowing what to expect ♦ Finding "right answers" ♦ Doing drills and assignment sheets ♦ Knowing exact expectations ♦ Getting quick and accurate feedback ♦ Being recognized for work well-done ♦ Being an active learner ♦ Having "hands-on" opportunities ♦ Seeing what to do (teacher modeling) ♦ Getting directions step by step Able to: Organize	Learns best by: ♦ Seeing how concepts relate to people ♦ Working with groups ♦ Sharing ideas ♦ Getting positive personal attention ♦ Role playing ♦ Learning about self, especially feeling. Able to: Empathize
Understanding Style	*Self-Expressive Style*
Learns best by: ♦ Analyzing situations ♦ Debating or arguing about ideas ♦ Working with other understanding style people ♦ Thinking and studying relationships among ideas. ♦ Carrying out projects that interest him/her. ♦ Solving problems that require inquiry and evaluation. Able to: Interpret	Learns best by: ♦ Multitasking ♦ Being creative ♦ Working with others on creative ideas ♦ Discussing open-ended questions and topics ♦ Discovering for himself/herself ♦ Having insight and awareness ♦ Thinking outside the box ♦ Organizing in his/her own way Able to: Create

See Chapter 3 on how to plan lessons using this concept.

Strategy 5—What Kind of Fruit Are You?

Katherine Butler (1987) has developed an engaging activity called "What Kind of Fruit Are You?" Students give themselves points in columns of descriptors to determine what kind of fruit they are. Grapes are imaginative, oranges are investigative, bananas are realistic, and melons are analytical. (This activity is found in Sean Covey, Jr.'s *Seven Habits of Effective Teens*, a great book to use to teach secondary students to be emotionally healthy.)

Directions: Read across each row and place a "4" in the blank for the word that best describes you. Now place a "3" in the blank for the second word that describes you best. Do the same for the final words using a "2" and a "1." Do this for each row. (The first row is an example.)

Imaginative	2	Investigative	4	Realistic	1	Analytical	3
Column One		Column Two		Column Three		Column Four	
Imaginative		Investigative		Realistic		Analytical	
Adaptable		Inquisitive		Organized		Critical	
Relating		Creating		Getting to the point		Debating	
Personal		Adventurous		Practical		Academic	
Flexible		Inventive		Precise		Systematic	
Sharing		Independent		Orderly		Sensible	
Cooperative		Competitive		Perfectionist		Logical	
Sensitive		Risk-taking		Hardworking		Intellectual	
People-person		Problem-solver		Planner		Reader	
Associate		Originate		Memorize		Think through	
Spontaneous		Charger		Wants direction		Judger	
Communicating		Discovering		Cautious		Reasoning	
Caring		Challenging		Practicing		Examining	
Feeling		Experimenting		Doing		Thinking	
Now add up your totals (don't include the example) for each column and place the totals in the blanks below							
Column One		Column Two		Column Three		Column Four	
Grape		**Orange**		**Banana**		**Melon**	

Find your fruit and see what it means to you on the next page.

What Does Your Fruit Mean to You?

	Grapes	*Oranges*	*Bananas*	*Melons*
Natural abilities include:	• being reflective • being sensitive • being creative • preference for working in groups	• experimenting • being independent • being curious • creating different approaches • creating change	• planning • organizing • fact finding • following directions	• debating points of view • analyzing ideas • finding solutions • determining value or importance
Can learn best when they:	• can work and share with others • balance work with play • can communicate • are noncompetitive	• can use trial and error • can compete • produce real products • are self-directed	• have an orderly environment • have specific outcomes • can trust others to do their parts • have predictable situations	• have access to resources • can work independently • are respected for intellectual ability • follow traditional methods
May have trouble	• giving exact answers • organizing • focusing on one thing at a time	• meeting time limits • having few options or choices • following a lecture	• understanding feelings • answering "what if" questions • dealing with opposition	• working in groups • being criticized • convincing others diplomatically
To expand their style they need to:	• pay more attention to details • be less emotional when making decisions • not rush into things	• delegate responsibility • be more accepting of others' ideas • learn to prioritize	• express their own feelings more • get explanations of others' views • be less rigid	• accept imperfection • consider others' feelings • consider all alternatives

Kathleen Butler has many publications and products. More information is available on Kathleen Butler's home page at http://www.learnersdimension.com

Step 4—Know Your Students Interests

Know what your students find interesting.

Finding out what your students are interested in is fairly simple if you employ these two strategies.

Strategy 1—Assign an Interests Essay

Ask your students to write you a letter or an essay about what interests them.

Strategy 2—Distribute the Interest Inventory

If you think their minds need prodding, use the following checklist to help them think.

Interest Inventory

Name: _____ Date: _____

Check all that apply to you. Put a star by things about which you are passionate (love a lot).

Sports

__ football   __ volleyball   __ golf   __ tennis

__ soccer   __ lacrosse   __ basketball   __ baseball

__ bowling   __ ping pong   __ track   __ snow skiing

__ water skiing   __ jogging   __ swimming   __ horseback riding

__ other (list: _____)

Hobbies

__ collecting things (what? _____)

__ playing an instrument (which one(s)?_____)

__ drawing   __ singing   __ acting   __ computer games

__ writing stories   __ writing poetry   __ pets   __ dancing

__ cooking   __ sewing   __ weaponry   __ archery

__ movie stars   __ rock stars   __ making things (what?_____)

Other Activities

__ talking on the telephone   __ shopping   __ bicycling   __ hiking

__ going to the opera   __ reading   __ going to movies   __ camping

__ going to orchestra concerts   __ going to dance concerts

__ going to plays   __ rock concerts or other music events

Societal Issues (of interest)

__ drug/alcohol abuse   __ abortion   __ teen pregnancy
__ race relations   __ poverty   __ busing

Medical Issues (of interest)

__ **STDs**   __ **juvenile diabetes**   __ **anorexia/bulimia**

__ cancer   __ heart disease   __ AIDs

Academic Subjects

__ history   __ math   __ literature   __ Environmental Studies

__ other: (List) _____

Psychology

__ Freud __ Jung   __Gestalt __Counseling Techniques

__ psychological testing   __dream analysis   __ hypnosis
__ psychotherapy techniques __psychiatry

Religion

__ **Jewish**   __ **Protestant**   __ **Catholic**   __ **Hindu**   __ **Islamic**

Countries

__ European—Which one(s)?_____
__ Asian—Which one(s)?_____
__ South American—Which one(s)?_____
__ Middle Eastern—Which one(s)?_____
__ African—Which one(s)?_____
__ Other—Which one(s)?_____

Animals

__ Which one(s)?_____

Education

__ Which level(s)?_____

In the space provided or on the back of this form, list any other interests you have and how you learn best.

Step 5—Find out about Students' Multiple Intelligences

Harold Gardner (1993) revolutionized teaching and learning when he posed the idea of "multiple intelligences." Although there exists no empirical proof that these intelligences exist, they have become recognized by most educators as reasonable and meaningful concepts by which to plan differentiated instruction.

The Eight Intelligences

Intelligence	Interests	Skills	Employment
Verbal/ linguistic	Stories, word play, grammar, writing styles	Reading, writing, speaking	Writer, public speaker, journalist, politician
Logical mathematical	Numbers, patterns, graphs, causes and effects, reasoning	Computation, deductive and inductive reasoning, seeing patterns, using methods of inquiry	Research scientist, engineer, computer technologist, accountant, economist
Spatial	Pictures, sculpture, film, visual puzzles	Painting, sculpting, filmmaking, making visual representations, solving visual puzzles	Visual artist, photographer, sculptor, tour guide, decorator, landscaper
Bodily Kinesthetic	Sports, dance, acting, touch, all kinds of movement, exercise	Athletic, dance, drama, hand–eye coordination, agility, muscle memory	Professional athlete, coach, dancer, actor, trainer
Musical	Singing, musical instruments, listening to music, learning songs	Song writing, singing, playing a musical instrument (at time by ear), going to musical performances	Singer, songwriter, composer, musician, music critic
Interpersonal	Talking to friends, doing things with groups, joining groups, serving on committees	Leading groups, counseling, planning parties and events, teaching	Teacher, therapist, administrator, counselor, manager, salesperson, politician

Intelligence	Interests	Skills	Employment
Intrapersonal	Self-analysis, writing in a journal, being on one's own	Knowing oneself, being OK without others around, set personal goals	Writer, editor, computer technician, scientist, philosopher
Naturalist	Ecology, environmental issues, hiking, canoeing, outdoor activities, rock climbing, gemology	Identifying and classifying plants and animals, enjoying nature to the fullest, saving the planet	Park ranger, ecologist, zoologist, veterinarian, hunter, scientist

Gardner, Harold, (1993) Multiple Intelligences: The Theory in Practice. New York: Basic Books.

Most people have more than one dominant intelligence. People who are brilliant in one intelligence usually do very well if they are allowed to pursue their interests and skills in that area. It is unfortunate that a weakness in the two critical intelligences could hinder the development of a natural ability. However, our society demands that every student develop "good enough" skills in reading, writing, and math or they are not considered educated; therefore, teachers should not let students get by with not developing those "good enough skills."

Find out which are your strongest intelligences, and then survey your students to find theirs. Use the checklist adapted from the Citizens Education Center. *Teaching and Learning through the Multiple Intelligences* ("Personal tour," 1994).

Multiple Intelligences Checklist

Name:_____ Date:_____

Check all the statements that apply to you. The *intelligence* with the greatest number of checks is the one in which you are most strong. Note: You may have more than one strong intelligence.

Linguistic Intelligence

__ Love to read

__ Hear words in my head before I read, speak, or write them down

__ Enjoy language: the potential to excite, persuade, inform, or entertain

__ Enjoy reading or writing poetry

__ Excel in English/Language Arts

__ Conversations frequently revolve around things I've read.

__ Enjoy doing crossword puzzles and playing games like SCRABBLE

__ Total Checks

Logical–Mathematical Intelligence

__ Can do mathematical operations in my head

__ Good at strategy games such as chess or checkers

__ Like to hypothesize and test my assumptions

__ Believe that most things have a rational explanation

__ Find logical flaws in things that people say and do

__ Will question persistently until I get an answer

__ Feel more comfortable when something is precise and can be measured

__ Total Checks

Visual–Spatial Intelligence

__ Often see clear visual images when I close my eyes

__ Enjoy solving jigsaw puzzles

__ Have vivid dreams with clear images and colors

__ Can find my way around in unfamiliar territory

__ For me, geometry is easier than algebra

__ Can interpret two dimensional drawings

__ Like to construct models

__ Total Checks

Bodily Kinesthetic Intelligence

__ Engage in sports, dance, or some other physical activity on a regular basis

__ Find it difficult to sit still for long periods of time

__ Like working with my hands: sewing, weaving, carving, carpentry, model building, or some similar activity.

__ Frequently use gestures, mime, and body language when conversing with someone

__ Need to touch things in order to learn more about them

__ Well coordinated

__ Need to practice a skill by doing it rather than reading about it or by watching a video

__ Total Checks

Musical Intelligence

__ Can tell when a musical note is off key

__ Frequently listen to music

__ Play a musical instrument

__ Can keep time to a piece of music

__ Know and like to sing many different songs or musical pieces and remember songs I have heard once or twice

__ Repeat songs and tunes in my head
__ Often make tapping sounds or sing melodies while working, studying, or learning something new
__ Total Checks

Interpersonal Intelligence

__ People come to me for advice or counsel, and I seek out others when I have a problem
__ Prefer spending time with others rather than alone
__ Have many close friends
__ Prefer group sports or activities
__ Enjoy the challenge of teaching others
__ Consider myself a leader
__ Like to be involved in social activities
__ Total Checks

Intrapersonal Intelligence

__ Need time alone to meditate, reflect, or think about important life questions
__ Have some important goals for my life that I think about on a regular basis
__ Have the will to carry out a project without much supervision
__ Can readily identify and express my own feelings
__ Have a strong sense of my inner self and seek opportunities for personal growth
__ Keep a diary or journal where I describe my feelings and values
__ Empathetic to the human condition and desire to make the world a better place through my actions
__ Total Checks

Naturalist Intelligence

__ Love to be outdoors
__ Know how to identify most plants and animals
__ Would rather be hiking and exploring than just about anything else
__ Feel safe and at home in the woods
__ Know how to use a compass and most equipment useful for outdoor activities
__ Care passionately about the environment
__ Do well in science class
__ Total Checks

Adapted from "A Personal Tour of Multiple Intellegences" (1994), Citizens Education Center, 310 First Avenue South, Suite 330, Seattle, WA 98104, 206-624-9955.

Step 6—Know Under What Conditions Students Learn Best

Find out under what conditions you and your students learn best. Then do all you can to create the optimum learning environment for yourself and your students. It sounds difficult, for instance some students may like a noisy environment whereas others want it quiet; however, here are some strategy suggestions.

Learning Preference	Strategy Suggestions
Noise	Let students who like noise bring CD players or tape players with ear phones, or play music for the whole class and let those who like it quiet wear ear plugs.
Light	Try to have a harsh light and soft light section of your classroom. If you have windows, students who like lots of light could sit near them. Lamps can help you develop softer lighting.
Time of Day	If you teach an early morning class, be aware that some of your students may not actually be awake when they are with you. Make sure your truly sleepy students have opportunities to do your work at home during their peak performance time. Make sure all students get a chance to do some key work during their peak performance times.
Temperature	Few teachers have very much control over the temperatures in their rooms. Suggest to students that they dress in layers so that they can adjust by modifying their own clothing.
Motivation	If you find a student or students who are chronically not motivated to do the work you assign, check the following in this order: (1) Does your style of presentation match their style of learning? (2) Is what you are teaching interesting enough for most students? (3) Is there something going on in the student's personal life that would interfere with motivation to do well in school?

Social Factors	Middle school students love to do group work because that is where they are developmentally. Group work is a "must" in the 90-minute block for middle school students. Most high school students also like group work, but not all of them feel that group grading is fair, and they are more affected by competition factors; therefore, teachers may want to allow individual work if any student prefers it (even a middle school student).
Classroom structure	If possible, have both rows of desks and an area that is less structured. If you have the luxury of a small class size, seminar style circles are wonderful. If your goal is student-to-student interaction, circles or semi-circles are a must. Rows are about teacher control.
Presentation Style	Lecture is going out of style, but if you want to teach your students to take good notes, you may need to teach them specific skills. If you want to assure that they will read those notes, you may want to ask them to do something with those notes other that "read" or "study" them. Cornell note-taking, a double entry note-taking style, is an excellent method because it requires students to develop questions about their notes. According to researchers, students' brains are more active when they are asking questions than when they are answering questions.
Sequencing Instruction	Based on brain-based research, the mind can only function well for fairly short periods of time. The time increases with age, but peaks at about 20 minutes in adulthood. Teachers cannot expect younger students, and students with focusing issues to do well for long periods; therefore, they should sequence their activities with planned breaks. These do not have to be literally breaks where students leave the classroom, but they could be breaks for reflection and discussion with a partner or small group. Students with longer attention spans can continue working through planned breaks if they choose.

To determine Learning Preferences, have students fill out this "Learning Preference Checklist."

Learning Preferences Checklist

Name:_____ Date:_____

Please check all that apply to you. Write a brief analysis of your strategy after each category.

Time of Day
___ I am a night owl.
___ I work best in the morning.
___ I work well at any time.
___ I get my best work done in the late afternoon.
Analysis:

Noise
___ I do better on an assignment if I can listen to music
___ I like to work with the television on.
___ I need complete quiet while I do school work.
___ I can learn in any environment.
Analysis:

Light
___ I need a lot of light when I learn—dim light distracts me.
___ I learn better when the light is dimmed and soft.
___ I can learn in harsh light or soft light.
Analysis:

Temperature
___ I cannot learn if I am too cold.
___ I cannot learn if I am too hot.
___ I am not sensitive to temperature.
Analysis:

Motivation
___ I am a self-starter—I do not need anyone to encourage me to begin working.
___ I need a push to get started on my work.
___ My parents are the ones who motivate me to study and learn.
___ My teachers motivate me to learn.
___ Some of my teachers turn me off to learning.
___ I am only interested in learning from certain teachers.
___ I am only interested in learning certain subjects.
___ I love to learn.
___ I want to go to college after high school.
___ I am not interest in college.

___ I know what I want to be when I am an adult. (What? _____
_____)

___ I have no idea what my future might be like.

___ I am willing to do my best in school to assure that I will be successful as an adult.

Analysis:

Social/Leadership

___ I like to study and learn with a friend or friends.

___ I prefer studying by myself.

___ I am a leader in my study group.

___ I am a leader in my class.

___ I do not like to answer questions in class.

___ Other students come to me for advice or help with school work.

Analysis:

Structure

___ I like to learn in a classroom that has desks in rows or other organized pattern.

___ I do not learn well when I have to sit in rows of desks. I need to be able to stretch out and be comfortable to learn.

___ I am highly organized.

___ I am not organized, but I get my work done and can find things when I need to.

___ I am not organized, and that is a problem for me. I need help to be more organized.

___ I do best if someone helps me focus on my work.

___ I need lots of concrete directions and modeling to understand an assignment or new concept.

___ I like to figure out things for myself.

___ I like to do things my way.

___ I need to take lots of notes when I am trying to learn.

___ I need to study without breaks.

___ I need lots of breaks when I study.

Analysis:

Time Management

Draw a circle and divide it to reflect your study time and your social time. You can include going to school as part of your study time. (Example: If you draw a line straight down the middle of your circle, you would be saying that you spend 50% of your time in each).

Analysis:

Add any other learning style strategies not covered by this check list:

Summarize how you learn best:

(Northey 2004)

Step 7—Know Where Your Students Are Developmentally

Make sure to review the stages of human growth and development, especially cognitive, psychosocial and physical development. Secondary level teachers become experts in the developmental needs of their students. For instance we know that when a student begins middle school he/she is going through tremendous cognitive, physical, and emotional changes.

What follows are some conceptualizations of the changes the average student goes through. Students who are developmentally delayed are usually considered to be "exceptional needs" students, and they need more than differentiation, they need accommodations (which are legally mandated for students with learning disabilities). Teachers should keep the developmental issues of their students in mind as they plan lessons for them.

Cognitive Development: Jean Piaget

Stage	*Age*	*Important Features of Development*
Concrete Operational	6/7 to 11/12	♦ Begin thinking logically ♦ Can reverse a process ♦ Can consider different perspectives ♦ Are concrete; think in terms of objects not concepts ♦ See the future as just an extension of the present ♦ Like to keep records ♦ See the world as stable enough for many views
Formal Operations	11/12 to Adult	♦ Have meta-cognitive abilities (i.e. can think about thinking) ♦ Can have idealistic views especially in early stages ♦ In early stages thinking can be highly critical because of contrast between idealism and reality ♦ Can think logically in abstract terms

From Ginn, W.Y (2003). Jean Piaget-Intellectual development. http://www.sk.com.br/sk-piage.htm.

Cognitive Development: Richard Paul
(Stages of Critical Thinking Development)

Richard Paul and Linda Elder (2001) believe that thinking can be taught and that there are six stages of Critical Thinking as follows: (1) unreflective thinker, (2) challenged thinker, (3) beginning thinker, (4) practicing thinker, (5) advanced thinker, (6) master thinker. Their book *Critical Thinking: Tools for Taking Charge of Your Learning and Your Life* has detailed information about improving your ability to think and solve problems.

Psychosocial Development: Erik Erikson

Stage	Ages	Basic Conflict	Summary
Latency	6–12	Industry vs. Inferiority	The child must begin school and learn to deal with the demands of learning new things and showing competence. The child risks the possibility of failure and appearing to be inferior to their peers.
Adolescence	12–18	Identity vs. Role Confusion	The teenager must develop a sense of identity in sex roles, occupation, politics, and religion.

Adapted from Erikson, E. H. (1950). *Childhood and Society.* New York: Norton.

Physical Development: Changes During Puberty

Stage	*Age Ranges*	*Girls' Changes*	*Boys' Changes*
1	Girls (8–11), Boys (9–12), Boys' Average Age:10 *Note*: For each stage, girls are slightly ahead of boys.	No outward signs of development, but ovaries are beginning to produce hormones.	No outward signs of development, but testicles are beginning to produce hormones. Some boys have a rapid growth rate at the end of this stage.
2	Girls (8–14), Average:11/12, Boys (9–15), Average: 12/13	Breast buds appear, height and weight increase, and first signs of pubic hairs are fine and straight.	Testicles and scrotum grow; very little, if any pubic hair begins to grow at the base of the penis; penis size does not increase very much.

Stage	Age Ranges	Girls' Changes	Boys' Changes
3	Girls (9–15), Average: 12/13, Boys (11–16), Average: 13/14	Breasts continue to grow; the vagina enlarges and produces a whitish discharge, which is cleansing; some girls begin menstrual periods late in this stage; pubic hair becomes coarser and thicker, but still not that thick.	Voice begins to deepen and crack; penis grows in length, but not width, pubic hair coarsens, thickens, and spreads toward the legs; height increases and facial features appear more adult; some hair begins to grow around the anus.
4	Girls (10–16), Average: 13/14, Boys (11–17), Average: 14/15	Pubic hair takes the triangular shape of adulthood, but still does not completely cover; underarm hair begins to grow, ovulation begins, but is not regular until stage 5.	Penis width and length increase; facial hair appears on chin and above upper lip; voice deepens; may have first ejaculations; underarm hair grows; pubic hair is similar to adult, but not as abundant; skin gets more oily.
5	Girls (12–19), Average: 15, Boys (14–18), Average: 16	Growth complete, physically an adult; breasts and pubic hair growth complete; ovulation and menstruation regular; full height is usually reached	Growth nearly complete; some boys develop more height and body hair (especially on chest) in early adulthood; pubic hair and genitals have adult appearance; facial hair is growing and shaving may begin

Adapted from J. Geoff Malta, M.A., Ed.M., NCC Adolescent Therapist, Puberty 101 Archives

Emotional Development

It is also important to know your students' Emotional Quotient (EQ). To determine each student's emotional development or issues, you may choose to do one of the following:

1. Have students self-assess their emotional strengths and weakness.
2. Consult students' cumulative folders and read any records that provide information about their emotional growth or issues.
3. Talk to a student's counselor if you suspect he/she is having significant emotional issues.
4. There are many Web sites that include online emotional intelligence tests and other resources. You may want to direct your students to www.EQ.org and/or www.eqi.org for interesting links and resources. I found an interesting EQ quiz online a few years ago and used it to discuss EQ with my students. It is no longer online, but there are many others from which to choose. Teen magazines are filled with quizzes and surveys about love and emotions. Students love assessing the emotional aspects of their lives, but they should understand that these assessments are not usually scientifically based, and therefore have no reliability or validity.

Emotional Intelligence: How Do You Rate?

Emotional Quotient (EQ) like Intelligence Quotient (IQ), is not an easily quantifiable measure. It pivots on such intangibles as social deftness, persistence, and empathy. Therefore, the quiz below is structured only to give you hints of your level of emotional intelligence; it is by no means definitive or foolproof. Give the test a whirl and see if you agree with its appraisal of your emotional quotient.

1. I'm aware of even subtle feelings as I have them.
    __always   __usually   __sometimes   __rarely   __never
2. I find myself using my feelings to help make big decisions in my life.
    __always   __usually   __sometimes   __rarely   __never
3. Bad moods overwhelm me.
    __always   __usually   __sometimes   __rarely   __never
4. When I'm angry, I blow my top or fume in silence.
    __always   __usually   __sometimes   __rarely   __never
5. I can delay gratification in order to reach goals instead of being carried away by impulses.
    __always   __usually   __sometimes   __rarely   __never

6. When I'm anxious about a challenge, such as a test or giving a speech, I find it difficult to prepare well.

__always   __usually   __sometimes   __rarely   __never

7. Instead of giving up in the face of setbacks or disappointments, I stay hopeful and optimistic.

__always   __usually   __sometimes   __rarely   __never

8. People don't have to tell me what they feel; I can sense it.

__always   __usually   __sometimes   __rarely   __never

9. My keen sense of others' feelings helps me understand how they are feeling.

__always   __usually   __sometimes   __rarely   __never

10. I have trouble handling conflict and emotional upsets in relationships.

__always   __usually   __sometimes   __rarely   __never

11. I can sense the way a group or individual is feeling and can identify unspoken feelings.

__always   __usually   __sometimes   __rarely   __never

12. I can soothe or contain distressing feelings so that they don't keep me from doing things I need to do.

__always   __usually   __sometimes   __rarely   __never

How to score:

Always = 4 points   Usually = 3 points
Sometimes = 2 points   Rarely = 1 point   Never = 0 points

Range:

37–44 points = **Excellent**
You have scored very well on this test, suggesting you excel in managing emotions, handling relationships effectively, and empathizing with others.

34–36 points = **Above Average**
Your emotional intelligence appears well-developed. You are probably productive and highly valued.

25–32 points = **Average**
Your grasp on emotional intelligence appears pretty good, but could use a little fine tuning.

22–24 points = **Low Average**
You probably realize you need to work on your emotional intelligence. That in itself is a good sign that you're on the road to improving it.

11–14 points = **Low**
You may need to reconsider some of your emotional habits. Fortunately, unlike IQ, emotional intelligence can be learned and developed.

Step 8—Know If Your Students Have "Exceptionalities"

Some students have been determined by scientifically-normed tests to be "Exceptional Children" (EC) or "Exceptional Learners" fall into categories beyond the scope of this book; however, I mention them here because many of the strategies I discuss are applicable to them. For one Exceptional Children's category, "Learning Disabled" (LD) student, teachers are required by law to adjust instruction and testing procedures to make accommodations for their specific disablility or disabilities. In contrast, "Regular Education" students must rely on their teachers to choose to differentiate instruction or not

Another group of "Exceptional Children" are those children who are labeled "Gifted and/or Talented." This book includes several strategies for students whose readiness levels might suggest that they are gifted, or at least advanced, in many or all elements of academic achievement. Strategies for the "Profoundly Gifted" are not included here, nor is there much detail about students who are "Twice Exceptional," for instance the LD *and* Gifted student; however, some of the strategies I explain can be adapted for these students.

Step 9—If Your Students Are Impoverished, You Need to Understand Them

A book by Ruby Payne (2001) taught me a great deal about a group of our children who seem very hard to reach. Here is some information adapted from this book

Behavior Related to Poverty	Intervention
Laugh when disciplined: A way to save face in matriarchal poverty	Understand the reason for the behavior. Tell students three or four other behaviors that would be more appropriate.
Argue loudly with the teacher: Poverty is participatory, and the culture has a distrust of authority. See the system as inherently dishonest and unfair.	Don't argue with the students. Have students write the answers to questions, such as "What did you do?" "When you did that, what did you want?" "List four other things you could have done." "What will you do next time?"
Angry response: Anger is based on fear. Question what the fear is: loss of face?	Respond in the adult voice (as opposed to child or parent voice). When students cool down, discuss other responses they could have used.
Inappropriate or vulgar comments: Reliance on casual register; may not know formal register.	Have students generate (or teach other students) phrases that could be used to say the same thing.
Physically fight: Necessary to survive in poverty. Only know the language of survival. Do not have language or belief system to use conflict resolution. See themselves as less than a man or woman if they do not fight.	Stress that fighting is unacceptable in school. Examine other options that students could live with at school other than fighting. One option is not to settle the business at school, for example.
Hands always on someone else: Poverty has a heavy reliance on non-verbal data and touch.	Allow them to draw or doodle. Have them hold their hands behind their back with in line or standing. Give them as much to do with their hands as possible in a constructive way.
Cannot follow directions: Little procedural memory used in poverty. Sequence not used or valued.	Write steps on the board. Have them write at the top of the paper the steps needed to finish the task. Have them practice procedural self-talk.

Behavior Related to Poverty	*Intervention*
Extremely disorganized: Lack of planning. Scheduling, or prioritizing skills not taught in poverty. Also probably don't have a place at home to put things so that they can be found.	Teach a simple, color-coded method of organization in the classroom. Use the five-finger method for memory at the end of the day. Have each student give a plan for organization.
Complete only part of a task: No procedural self-talk. Do not "see" the whole task.	Write on the board all the parts of the task. Require each student to check off each part when finished.
Disrespectful to teacher: Have a lack of respect for authority and the system. May not know any adults worthy of respect.	Tell students that disrespect is not a choice. Identify for students the correct voice tone and word choices that are acceptable. This allows students to practice.
Harm other students verbally or physically: This may be a way of life. Probably a way to buy space or distance. Poverty tends to address issues in the negative.	Tell students that aggression is not a choice. Have students generate other options that are appropriate at school. Give students alternate phrases to those used.
Cheat or steal: Indicative of weak support system, weak role models and/or weak emotional resources. May indicate extreme financial need. May indicate little instruction/guidance during formative years.	Use a metaphor story to find the reason or need behind the cheating or stealing. Address the reason or need. Emphasize that the behavior is illegal and not an option at school.
Talk incessantly: Poverty is very participatory.	Have students write all questions and responses on a note card two days a week. Tell students that each gets five comments a day. Build participatory activities into the lesson.

From: Payne, Ruby K. (2001). A Framework for Understanding Poverty. Highlands, TX: aha! Process, Inc.

Step 10—Documenting What You Know

You should keep at least one page on each of your students documenting key facts about them. Here is a "Differentiation Data Sheet" that may used as it is or adapted to meet your needs.

Differentiation Data Sheet (Confidential)

Completed by the teacher as information is available.

Date Begun: _____

Name:_____ Date of Birth:_____ Age:_____

Family Information (Check one):

__In tact __Divorced (single parent) __Blended(step parents)
__Other (explain on back)

List names and ages of brothers and sister (if applicable):

Socioeconomic Status: __free/reduced lunch __no free/reduced lunch

Other economic considerations (if applicable):

Exceptionalities:

__Certified Gifted __ADD __ADHD __Mental Health Issues (List):_____
__Certified Learning Disabled (list disabilities): _____

Reading Level:

__well below grade level   __below grade level   __at grade level
__ above grade level   __well above grade level
How was this level determined?_____

Favorite Learning Mode: __Auditory   __Visual   __Haptic

Learning Environment Preferences:

__noise   __quiet   __light (high)   __light (dim)
__temperature (high)   __temperature (low)
__formal classroom structure   __informal classroom structure

Teacher-Student Relationship

__ excellent   __average   __below average   __poor

Parent-Student Relationship

__excellent   __average   __below average   __poor

Cognitive Development

__Normal Stage of Cognitive Development   __Delayed Stage of Cognitive Dev.

Critical Thinking Ability   **Motivation to Learn—Level:**

_____Thinker   __Exceptional __Average __Below Average __Poor

Physical Development

___Stage of Puberty   Comments: _____

Multiple Intelligence

__Linguistic   __Logical/Mathematical   __Bodily Kinesthetic   __Spatial
__Musical   __Interpersonal   __Intrapersonal   __Naturalist

Interests (list): _____

Emotional Quotient

__emotionally mature   __emotionally average   __emotional issues (explain):

Socially

__a group leader   __likes to work in groups   __gets off task in groups

__likes to work alone

(Northey 2003)

Summary

Obviously, it is unreasonable for middle school and high school teachers to administer differentiation assessments in all of their classes. Time would be wasted and students would rebel. Therefore, individual schools or school districts could develop procedures for efficiently collecting differentiation data on their student bodies. For instance, homeroom teachers could be responsible for administering differentiation assessments on students who are in their homerooms. They could also be responsible for completing a "Differentiation Data Sheet" (DDS) for each of their homeroom students. The first year a student enters a school, the DDS should be initiated. In following years, homeroom teachers could revise/update the DDS. Homeroom teachers and/or counselors could file the DDSs in students' cumulative files/folders. All teachers would have access to the information; in the event that they are having difficulty meeting a student's learning needs the DDS could be an excellent resource for adjusting instruction.

There are many things to understand about yourself and your many students. I have given you a few tools to use and concepts to think about. However, the most important idea from this chapter is that if you help your students become advocates for their own learning, they will learn to accurately choose

- their best learning environment,

- their best way of showing they know content and skills,

- their best way to learn content or skills, and

- the most appropriate resources to help them learn.

The other important concept is that you need to make certain to provide these choices for your students as best you can.

2

Gathering Resources (Content Differentiation)

When you know who your students are, the next step involves developing materials, finding resources and organizing those resources to meet their needs. Most teachers have two sources of content information: their textbooks and enrichment materials.

Textbooks

There are two possibilities regarding differentiating textbooks; either or both are useful to differentiate content.

- Provide **textbooks** that are on a grade level close to students' actual reading level.

  Find an alternate text for those students reading well-below the grade level of your primary content source. Globe Fearon has a great selection of high-interest, low–reading level textbooks for a variety of content areas: social studies, language arts, math, and science. If you teach English/Language Arts, novels with lower Lexile levels are available as well as easy to read, high-interest novel sets from Globe-Fearon and other publishers.

  My hope is that someday school districts will provide all of the resources teachers need to teach to the reading needs of all students. If your district does not provide funds to purchase these resources in the regular education setting, attempt to borrow from the Exceptional Children's department in your school.

- Make the textbook more readable by **providing "scaffolding"** (a temporary cognitive support system) for students who cannot access information by reading your textbook.

There are several scaffolding strategies that take some time to develop, but make your textbook more readable for your below grade level readers. Scaffolding is a term used to describe the temporary cognitive support teachers use to help students who are struggling with a concept or skill until they become more proficient in understanding that concept or performing that skill on their own. There are many more strategies than are described here; however, those strategies described here have stood the test of time and constitute some of the "Best Practices" in differentiation and general classroom instruction.

Scaffolding Activities

One of the most important ways teachers help students access information through their textbooks is by implementing meaningful and engaging reading "scaffolding" activities. First, teachers should use **prereading** activities that prepare the brain for receiving information. Both prior knowledge and the affective domain must be engaged if learning is to take place. Teachers waste precious time if they do not make time to get students ready to read. Next, they should also use **during reading** strategies to model accomplished reader behavior and comprehension skills. Finally, they should use **after reading** strategies to check for understanding and demonstrate that students have read for a purpose. Here are some essential reading strategies:

Prereading Activities

Strategy 1—Teach Students to Access Prior Knowledge

The KWL Chart

It is very important to use this activity. If students are to build new knowledge, it must be attached to a prior knowledge source in their brains. Asking students what they already know about a topic or concepts allows this process to begin. Also asking students what they want to learn helps them "buy into" the process of learning about the topic or concept. Determining what they have learned is a critical step in the process that tells the teacher what to reteach and when to move on to the next topic or concept.

How to Use this Chart:

When beginning a topic or unit of study, draw this chart on the board or have an already drawn chart ready to go. (You may want to laminate a chart so that you may reuse it.) Put the topic on the board and ask students what they know about it. Write all reasonable ideas in the **K** column (What Students Know). Next, ask students what they would like to learn about the topic. For instance, what questions do they have about that topic. Write what students want to learn in the **W** column (What Students Want to Learn). As you finish each day, you could add information to the **L** column (What Students have Learned) or you could wait until the end of the unit to review what students have learned. Example:

Topic—The Digestive System

K (What Students Know)	W (What Students want to Learn)	L (What Students Learned)
◆ Stomach ◆ Food ◆ Eating ◆ Upset stomach ◆ Stomach virus	◆ What organs are in the digestive system? ◆ How does the stomach work? ◆ What foods are easy to digest? ◆ Where do stomach viruses come from? ◆ What upsets the stomach?	◆ The organs in the digestive system are: the mouth, esophagus, stomach, small intestine, large intestine, rectum, and anus. ◆ Enzymes help the digestive system digest food. ◆ Etc.

Author note: Some teachers add an **H** column (How I want to learn it). There are a wealth of graphic organizers, including several ways of adapting the basic KWL chart, in a book by Pattie Tarquin and Walker Sharon (1997) *Creating Success in the Classroom: Visual Organizers and How to Use Them.*

Strategy 2—Teach Students to Use the Patterns of Informational Text

As students prepare to read information from their textbooks, point out organizational patterns that will prepare their minds to absorb the information they are going to read. Learning the skills of identifying text structures helps students remember information better and helps them distinguish major concepts from less important ones.

Talk to students about subtitles, captions, and signal words that will help them create meaning as they read. Use basic reading comprehension terms as you share reading with them. Remember, however, that most secondary level students are fully aware of text structure; therefore, you might avoid giving this information except as review for most students. Help struggling students practice identifying text aids to facilitate comprehension.

Here is a simple chart to share with your students as a review. Or use it as a guide to help struggling students practice preparing their minds to grasp important and often brand new concepts from informational texts:

Patterns of Informational Text

Pattern of Organization	Definition	Signal Words	Example
Cause and Effect	The interaction between two events or ideas in which the action of one results in the other.	◆ therefore ◆ since ◆ because ◆ as a result	Because of severe flooding, the farmers did not make their usual income for the year.
Compare and Contrast	Shows apparent similarities and differences.	◆ but ◆ on the other hand ◆ however ◆ either…or ◆ as well as ◆ not only	Plant cell mitosis is similar to animal cell mitosis however plant cells form spindle fibers but do not have centrioles.
Time Order	Demonstrates a sequence of events over a specified time	◆ before ◆ now ◆ later ◆ after	Martin Luther was a critic of the practices of the Catholic church. In 1517, he wrote 95 statements attacking church practices. Later he was excommunicated. While in hiding, he translated the Bible from Latin into German.
Problem/ Solution	Cites a problem and offers a solution. This is similar to cause and effect.	◆ therefore ◆ since ◆ because ◆ as a result	Laws in the south prohibited slaves from owning property, reading, marrying, or buying their own freedom. Despite these laws, slaves managed to develop a sense of community and a culture. One way they were able to develop that culture was through story telling.

Strategy 3—Teach Students Key Vocabulary Words

Vocabulary development is essential for struggling readers. Here are a few of the best methods to use in "Prereading." The next section presents others to use "During Reading."

Author note: For a fuller discussion of how to teach new words for differentiating instruction, see of Amy Benjamin's *Differentiated Instruction: A Guide for Middle and High School Teachers* (Chapter 6, page 75).

Word Cards

This strategy helps students learn the meanings and relationships of words they will encounter as they read their textbook. You should use this strategy before students read.

The teacher should create a list of key vocabulary words from the text, and then write these terms on the board or a transparency. Students should copy these words onto cards and write their definitions. Next the teacher should ask the students to group the vocabulary words based on how they are related to one another. They may begin by creating three or more groups of related words. Students may use their groups to construct a concept map using linking words.

The following vocabulary strategies are featured in *Teaching Reading in the Content Areas* by Rachel Billmeyer and Mary Lee Barton:

Concept Mapping

This strategy is useful when merely looking up a word in the dictionary does not tell enough about what the word really means. Teach students to make a graphic organizer for a word that includes the answers to questions like: What is it? What is it not? What larger category might it fit under? What are some examples of it? What are its important characteristics? What makes it different from other concepts that are like it (e.g., its connotations)? Use an already known concept to model how to do this before asking students to do it on their own. After the students complete their maps, ask them to write a comprehensive definition of the word. This strategy would only be used for difficult, but key, concepts that students should fully explore (Schwartz, 1988). Example:

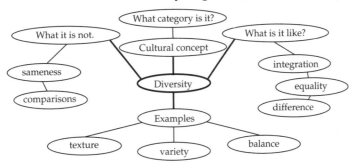

Hilda Taba's Model of Concept Development

Hilda Taba's (1967) model uses Bruner's, Goodnow's, and Austin's (1967) ideas of concept attainment (inductive reasoning) to help students define difficult content concepts. She believed that teachers could help students move past developmental limitations by using her complex method of concept attainment. The process can be lengthy and at times frustrating, but it is well worth the effort if you have a concept in your content area that needs to be fully defined so that students may understand subsequent concepts and information.

Here are the basic steps (for further information go to www.lovinlearning. com or to www.google.com for more resources):

- Step 1: Teacher puts a complex concept on the board or on a flip chart. Example "Diversity."

- Step 2: Teacher asks students to brainstorm a list of words that come to mind when they see that word. Teacher records all answers. No idea is wrong!

- Step 3: Teacher asks students to group words from the list in many ways, and to find three labels for each group. This step is tricky. Help students make sentences with stems (such as: "They are alike because they are both….") to help them name the groups.

    Example: black/white They are alike because they are both skin colors; They are alike because they can be symbolic; and They are alike because they are both extremes of color. Group labels: skin colors, symbols, extremes of color.

    Teacher records all groupings.

- Step 4: Looking at labeled groupings of words and how they are alike, the teacher asks students to determine categories that might be subsumed under other categories. Example: "skin colors," "hair styles," "body types" could be subsumed under "Physical Attributes."

    Teacher records all groupings.

- Step 5: This step seems like overkill, but it is very important. Ask students to repeat step 2 to step 4 making completely different groupings and labels.

    Teacher records new groupings. This step deepens students' understanding of the concept. I had to see it to believe it, but it's true.

Frayer Model

This graphic model also helps students learn new words by asking them to discover the relational aspects of words. This organizer is useful only for difficult but key concepts in the unit.

Write the *word* in a *circle* in the middle of the chart.

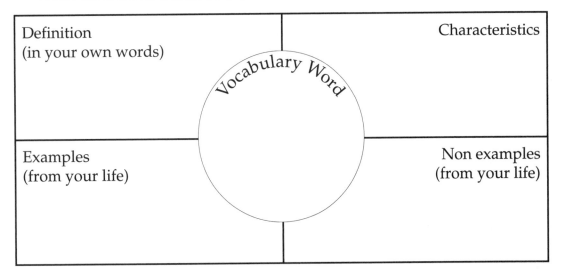

An adaptation of this model is to draw a picture in one of the boxes.

From Frayer,D. A., Frederick, W. C., and Klausmeier, H. G. (1969). A schema for testing the level of concept mastery." In Technical Report No. k16. Copyright 1969 by the University of Wisconsin.

Other Ideas

Here are some other ideas about teaching vocabulary skills.

Introduce key vocabulary related to the specific concepts included in a content-area

- ◆ Examine relationships among the words to form categories to help students make connections.
- ◆ Point out root words, prefixes, and suffixes.
- ◆ Provide direct instruction on selected words.
- ◆ Model a "think-aloud" process for students.
- ◆ Encourage and guide students to create their own vocabulary list.
- ◆ Link and integrate new and unfamiliar words to existing knowledge of words.
- ◆ Consider any academic, ethnic, religious, and cultural backgrounds of students that may affect content priorities in relationship to word meaning.

♦ Utilize organizational patterns in text (text structure) that may help students with new words.

♦ Determine expectations for students' learning in relation to word meaning skills.

♦ Develop instructional strategies to link word meaning with meta-cognition, prior knowledge, inferencing, and text structure strategies.

♦ Select critical vocabulary and develop a plan to link that vocabulary to concepts and other content areas.

♦ Select appropriate graphic organizers to reinforce learning (such as "Thinking Maps," see Strategy 7, Idea 2 for more information).

Strategy 4—Teach Students How to Read Informational Text

Anticipation Guide/Prediction Guide

This strategy can be used to access prior knowledge, focus reading, and stimulate students' interest in a topic. Take the following steps: (1) Identify an important concept from a unit of study. (2) Determine which concepts might support or challenge students' beliefs about the topic. (3) Write 4 to 6 challenging remarks that address important concepts related to the topic of study. Make sure the statements are not literal or easy. (4) Students can work in groups or individually to react to the statements you have written. (5) Discuss the statements as a class. Find who agreed and who disagreed with each statement. (6) Ask students to read from the text to find support for their points of view. (7) Encourage students to change statements that are not true. (8) Discuss findings as a class. Example:

Anticipation Guide

Directions: In the column labeled "Me" put a check by all statements with which you agree. As you read the text, put a check by the statements that are true. Compare the checks in your column with the checks in the "text" column. Rewrite false statements to make them true.

Me   Text   Statements

___   ___   1.   Canada is more like the United States than Great Britain.

___   ___   2.   More people move from the United States to Canada than from Canada to the United States.

___   ___   3.   There are relatively few native Canadians compared to the number of immigrants that arrive each year.

___   ___   4.   The government of Canada is just like the government in the United States.

Direct Reading/Thinking Activity

Similar to KWL, this strategy asks students to make predictions, activate prior knowledge, and check out the accuracy of their predictions.

Ask student to read and fill in the following organizer.

Directed Reading/Thinking Activity
What I know I know.
What I think I know.
What I think I'll learn
What I know I learned

Strategy 5—Engage the Affective Domain (i.e., the Emotions)

It is highly important to get students emotionally involved with the topic. Once again I can't say enough about engaging students' attention to reading the text by getting them affectively involved in what they are about to read. Brain-based research has shown without a doubt that engaging the affective domain increases learning. Students cannot learn if they are under too much stress. Students must feel intellectually safe in order to learn. Here are two activities to engage learners:

Philosophical Chairs

Take these steps:

- ◆ Pose a controversial statement related to your topic of study.
- ◆ Ask students to take one side or the other.
- ◆ Ask students who agree with the statement to go to one side of the room and those who take the opposing view to go to the other side.
- ◆ Have a designated chair on each side from which students may speak.
- ◆ Only the student in the chair may speak.
- ◆ Sides take turns speaking.
- ◆ As speakers make their points, students may change sides. They may change sides as often as they like.

If the statement is really well formed, the spilt will be good and the debate will elicit students' affective involvement in the topic or concept.

This strategy is useful in all content areas. Here is an example from each:

Social Studies:

No culture should be allowed to make laws that give men more rights than women.

Science:

Scientists should continue to explore ways to genetically engineer life.

English/Language Arts:

Writers should be held accountable for the negative impact they might have on innocent young people.

Math:

If you can solve a problem correctly in your head, there is no reason to show your work.

Find the most controversial and timely issues from your content area, and then formulate a statement that will have two obvious and opposing views.

What If? Questions

Asking "what if?" questions engage students' imagination and their emotions. Posing an interesting "what if?" question can be an excellent way to start a class or unit of study.

Social Studies:

What if in a given election, some people were allowed to vote multiple times based on their status in society?

Science:

What if it rained non-stop for 40 days?

English/Language Arts:

What if you were in charge of the banned books list in our school?

Math:

What if 0 didn't exist?

Strategy 6—Engage All Learners: Experiential Activities

Any activity related to the topic that is "hands on" and gets students moving and reacting is worth developing or finding in resource books. Often the primary source will have suggestions of "hands on" activities to start a class or a unit. Example:

This is a Mini Lab that you will do with a partner. Using two colors of counters (blue and red). Problem: Find the sum of 7+(-4) using the counters.

Do This:

- ◆ One color counter should stand for the positive numbers and the other color should stand for the negative numbers. Suggestion: Red represents positive and Blue represents negative.
- ◆ Put 7 positive and 4 negative counters on a sheet of paper.
- ◆ When the positive counter is pared with the negative counter, the result is a "zero pair." Because a zero pair has a value of zero, you can add or remove zero pairs without changing the value of the set. Remove all zero pairs from the paper.
- ◆ The counters you have left represent the solution.

Questions to answer:

♦ Is the sum of 7+(-4) negative or positive?

♦ What number (7 or -4) has the greater absolute value?

♦ Use the counters to find the sum of -7 +4 = t. Compare the sign of the sum to the sign of the number with the greater absolute value.

♦ Make a conjecture about the sign of the sum -10+4 = m

From *Mathematics: Applications and Connections: Course 3*, 1999.

Strategy 7—Use Brain Gym: A Resource for Kinesthetic Learners

Most teachers are familiar with resources to address visual and auditory learning styles; however, they have not typically had a wealth of resources to address kinesthetic learning styles. Teachers who wish to differentiate for kinesthetic learners may be interested in the field of Educational Kinesiology (the study of posture and movement to address learning). An interesting strategy that implements the concept of Educational Kinesiology is called *Brain Gym*. You can find out more about it by going to (www.braingym.org). It is an interesting resource for exercises that purport to stimulate kinesthetic learners and other learners to think more clearly and to perform at higher levels.

Brain Gym exercises are best learned in training sessions; however, you can learn some exercises from the book *Brain Gym* by Dr. Paul E. and Gail E. Dennison. These exercises are adapted from the work of Carla Hannaford, Ph.D., a neurophysiologist and educator for over 28 years. In her book, *Smart Moves,* she explains how the body and the brain work together in a network that contributes to our intelligence and capacity to learn. Brain Gym can easily be implemented in any classroom according to its authors.

"During Reading" Strategies

Strategy 1—Teach Students to Identify Vocabulary Words as They Read

Quadruple-Entry Word Journal

When you assign students to read something (a novel, a chapter in their textbook), ask them to keep a record of words they don't know in the context of what they are reading. Help them focus on understanding the word in context, and by writing an example, synthesizing the definition with its relevant connotations. Example:

Quadruple-Entry Word Journal

for _____ (title of book or source)

Word	Sentence (Page # on which the sentence appears)	Definition	Example (Focus on connotations-usage of the word)
polygon	p. 357	A simple, closed figure in a plane formed by three or more sides.	Artists use polygons to create interesting patterns.

Strategy 2—Choose from among Eight Oral Reading Strategies (Wood, 1992): A Resource for Auditory Learners

Oral reading is alive and well in the secondary classroom. Even though "Round Robin Reading " (the technique in which the teacher calls upon students randomly to read the text to the class) has proved to have little benefit for either comprehension or engagement of readers, there are several worthwhile strategies that help struggling readers *hear* the text. Here is a list of "During Reading" strategies that seem to work:

♦ Pairs Read (1)

- Choose a selection (e.g., a chapter) for students to read.

- Ask students to choose a partner (or the teacher can pair students).

- Student 1 reads a paragraph from the selection to student 2.

- Student 2 summarizes the main idea and supportive details from the paragraph student 1 just read. Student 2 can ask student 1 to help remember points if necessary.

- The students reverse roles and follow the same procedure.

- Students continue alternating roles until they finish the selection

♦ Pairs Read or Paired Reading (2): The teacher randomly calls on two students to read the text in unison for the class.

♦ Choral Reading: All students read together. Use this one for special reading passages like poems.

♦ Cloze Reading: Teacher reads the text and stops before a word. The teacher calls on a student to supply the next word.

♦ Mumble Reading: Students mumble the words as they read. This strategy could be used for selected passages, but not for a long period of time (Cunningham, 1978).

♦ Whisper Reading: Teachers can ask partners or whole groups to whisper the words from the text.

♦ Imitation Reading: The teacher could read a section of the text, and then ask a student to read the same text. This is especially useful for dialogue, when expression is helpful for comprehension.

♦ 4-Way Reading (Wood, 1983): The teacher asks students to use a variety of the strategies listed here. She/he may ask the students to *cloze* read, then move into mumble reading, followed by whisper reading, and finally into reading with a partner or choral reading. The teacher leads the class somewhat like a chorus leader leads the chorus, which can make for a very lively reading experience for everyone.

Strategy 3—Use Teacher Modeling

"Think-Aloud"

Teachers model metacognitive skills for students as they read a text.
Steps:

♦ Explain that reading is a matter of creating meaning and that as you read your mind is filled with questions that help you understand what you are reading.

♦ Select a passage to read aloud that contains sections that could be hard to understand.

♦ Teacher reads aloud while students follow silently. As the teacher reads, she verbalizes her own questions and models how she creates meaning for herself from the text.

Some strategies:

• Talk about what you "see" as you read. Example: When the author describes the sunset, I can see the beautiful colors and remember the times I have enjoyed sunsets at the beach.

• Make predictions about what you think will happen next: chronologically or conceptually. Example: I can tell by the way the writer is describing how cold it is getting that it will probably begin to snow.

- Show how you connect new information with prior knowledge. When the writer talks about the nutritional value of fresh fruits, I can remember learning that vitamin C helps the body deal with colds.

- Create analogies. When I read about the guilds from medieval times, I think about the trade unions of today.

- Talk about trouble spots, such as difficult vocabulary words that you have to know. Talk students through strategies like rereading the passage or asking the teacher for help.

Students can assess their ability to use "think-aloud" strategies:

Evaluate your use of these strategies as you read.

Strategy	Not much	A little	Often	All the time
Making and revising predictions				
Forming mental pictures				
Connecting to prior knowledge				
Acknowledging confusing places in the text				
Use fix-up strategies				

Strategy 4—Create Study Guides for Difficult Texts

Study guides that require students to answer questions as they read the text are valuable to help students understand difficult text. They take some time to develop, but they often provide the best way a student can understand what he/she is reading.

Strategy 5—Use a Levels Guide

A levels guide is an engaging method to get students to focus on the text and the diagrams/pictures in their primary resource or textbook.

Example from *Science Voyages Grade 6*. 2000.

Chapter 15.1 Level Guide (pp. 414–421):
Energy Changes

Level I Directions: Read each statement carefully. Using your textbook, decide if the statement is true or false. If the statement is true, place a check mark in the first blank and the page number of the statement in the second blank. If the statement is false, put a "0" in the first blank and the page number in the second blank. Correct all statements that are false so that you have true statements to help you study for your test.

True "✓"   Page
False "0"

____	____	1.	Energy is the ability to cause change.
____	____	2.	Energy come in many forms.
____	____	3.	Energy often changes from one form to another.
____	____	4.	During energy transformations, the total amount of energy stays the same. Only the form of energy changes.
____	____	5.	Energy can take many forms such as light, heat, and motion.
____	____	6.	Objects in motion have a type of energy called kinetic.
____	____	7.	The amount of kinetic energy depends on the color and the speed of the object.
____	____	8.	Potential energy is energy that comes from position or condition.
____	____	9.	There is a direct relationship between the amount of potential energy an object has and the amount of energy that can be transformed into kinetic energy.
____	____	10.	Kinetic energy can be transferred from one object to another when those objects collide.
____	____	11.	According to the laws of conservation of energy, energy cannot be created or destroyed.

Level II Directions: Go back to the beginning of the chapter and repeat the process, paying close attention to the pictures, charts, and diagrams. Follow the same procedure to mark the blanks and remember to correct all false statements.

True "✓"   Page
False "0"

____   ____   12.   According to Figure 15-1, energy allows the riders of the skateboard and bike to change their speed and direction.

____   ____   13.   According to Figure 15-2, fireworks result when chemical energy of the fireworks material is changed to light, sound, and heat energy.

____   ____   14.   From Figure 15-3, the water that is held back by the dam is higher than the water in the river below the dam. The water that is held behind the dam has potential energy.

____   ____   15.   According to Figure 15-4, you must consider both masses and speeds of the objects. The train must have more kinetic energy than the skater.

____   ____   16.   Figure 15-5 shows us that the skier at the top of the ski run has the least amount of potential energy.

____   ____   17.   According to Figure 15-5, we can see that potential energy changes to kinetic energy as the skier begins to ski down the slope.

____   ____   18.   Figure 15-6 shows an amusement park ride. At the top of the swing, the ride has the greatest amount of potential energy and the least amount of kinetic energy.

____   ____   19.   According to Figure 15-7, when you tap the dominoes and they start falling against one another, potential energy is changed to kinetic energy.

Level III Directions: Using your prior knowledge and what you have learned from this section, write a paragraph that explains what happens with potential energy and kinetic energy as you ride a roller coaster.

Strategy 6—Assign Double Entry or Two Column Note-Taking and Journaling

A double entry journal is a two-column structure to help students organize their thinking.

See three types—A, B, and C—as examples:

A. Use a double entry or two-column note-taking strategy in which students write one type of information on the right side of the text and another kind on the left side. See the five examples below:

Double Entry or Two-Column Notes (Examples)

Main Idea The 5 themes of geography	*Supporting Details* ♦ Location ♦ Place ♦ Region ♦ Movement ♦ Human-environment interaction
Compare Active Immunity and Passive Immunity: They both fight disease by forming antibodies	*Contrast* Active immunity occurs when the body makes its own antibodies and passive immunity is when antibodies produced in another animal are introduced into the body. Passive immunity does not last as long as active immunity.
Opinion Adverb clauses make sentences more interesting	*Proof* (or Fact) An adverb clause should be followed by a comma when it comes before an independent clause.
Vocabulary Translation	*Definition* In math: A sliding motion
Problem Traffic accident report	*Solution* Use square roots, real numbers, and distance on a coordinate plane to draw a diagram in order to determine what actually happened.

B. Use Cornell note-taking strategy (Paulk, 1984) as follows: Students take notes from the text on the right side of a page. After they have taken notes on an entire chapter or discrete section of a text, they should go back, read their notes, and then develop questions from those notes.

Cornell Notes

Questions	Notes
What kinds of people were native to the Western Hemisphere? What is the surviving evidence of their civilization? What else was going on in the world around the 11th and 13th centuries? What is unique about the Anasazi civilization?	◆ Native Americans were the first people to inhabit the Western Hemisphere. ◆ They came to North America from Eastern Asia, 12,000 to 35,000 years ago. ◆ The Mississippians and the Anasazi developed complex civilizations. ◆ The height of the Anasazi civilization was around 11th to 13th centuries. ◆ They built homes called cliff dwellings that had from 20 to 1,000 rooms. ◆ These remains can be seen in the Mesa Verde National Park in Colorado and in other places in the Southwestern United States.

Author note: The question-writing phase is best done as homework because it requires students to review what they have read, and it is more likely that students will focus on the information so that they can understand it and recall it better.

C. Use a **double entry journal** that requires students to reference the text (concrete information) on the left and analyze the text (abstract information on the right). To get students started, you might want to fill in parts of the journal and ask them to fill out the other parts. You might want to start by filling in the abstract side first and then the concrete. The goal is for them to be able to fill out both sides by themselves.

Here is an example from *House of the Seven Gables* (Hawthorne, 2000):

Concrete	*Abstract*
Quote the words of phases from the novel that reflect the author's tone(s).	Tone 1: mysterious Tone 2: foreboding
Symbol 1: Colonel Pyncheon's portrait Symbol 2: the house of the seven gables Symbol 3: the mirror	Explain what each symbolizes.
Find a sentence that is difficult to understand	Explain its meaning.
Write your favorite sentence that contains a literary device.	Interpret the sentence.

Strategy 7—For Visual/Spatial Learners

Idea 1: Use Graphic Organizers

Graphic organizers are an excellent means to help visual/spatial learners organize their thinking. They also help students who are overwhelmed by information imbedded in paragraphs "see" how concepts fit together. These organizers can actually help some students' minds retrieve and understand information. I have already mentioned that the book of graphic organizers by Tarquin and Walker (in KWL charts) can be helpful for most learners.

Idea 2: Use Thinking Maps

Dr. David Hyerle's (2000) "Thinking Maps" purport to actually improve access to higher level thinking skills for students. You can go online to learn about how to teach the eight different "Thinking Maps" conceptualized by Hyerle and promoted by the "Innovative Learning Group." For more information: www.mapthemind.com (Dr. Hyerle's official Web site) and/or http:www.thinkingmaps.com.

Idea 3: Use Mind Maps for Organizing as You Read

Tony Buzon (1996) has proposes that "mind maps" can actually map the way the brain is thinking. He suggests the following process for students to use in order to create these maps:

- Step 1: Be relaxed and count on having fun. Don't be critical of yourself or others. Work quickly no more than 5 to 7 minutes at a time. You may think of words and ideas too fast to write them all down.

- Step 2: Put a colored main image in the center of your map.

- Step 3: Draw lines out from the main image and print key words on those lines. You can also use images and symbols. Each line should be connected getting closer to the center. The most important ideas are closer to the center. Each new line you draw should leave room for more connections and subideas that might be farther from the center.

- Step 4: Use colors to help you organize your thoughts. Make sure these colors please your eyes.

  Mind Mapping is a great way to organize your thinking so that you can remember what you want to remember. Go to http://webits3. appstate.edu./apples/study/Creativity/new_page_19.htm for more information about this great idea.

"After Reading" Strategies

The easiest activity to use after reading is for students to ask and/or answer questions about what they have just read. The process can be an oral one using a seminar or other kind of whole class interactive discussion, or it can be a written assignment asking students to write short answers or longer compositions about the text. Other whole class activities include the following: taking students on a field trip that supports the unit, conducting a trial about the topic, or having a debate or other structured conversation about the text. Teachers could also ask students to choose from a wide variety of individual, partner, or group projects that require them to show their understanding of the text. Here is a list of my favorite types of projects or activities after reading:

- Make a documentary
- Do a skit
- Make puppets to act what happened in the text
- Draw a picture or pictures that symbolize or represent what has been read
- Make a children's game
- Make a collage
- Make up a rap song or other song
- Act out a talk show
- Interview characters or major figures from a topic

- Do a tableau of a scene
- Make a one minute speech
- Make a sculpture or model
- Make a diorama
- Make a map
- Make a "mouse" journal (a miniature journal)
- Make a timeline
- Make a story map or story board
- Make a comic book version
- Dress up like a person from the text
- Express the perspective of a person or character from the text
- Choreograph and perform a dance that demonstrates a concept or story
- Write a futuristic version or an ancient version
- Use new vocabulary words to create a story
- Make up a mnemonic device
- Make a poster
- Make a commercial
- Make an advertisement
- Write an editorial
- Write a poem
- Have a contest (e.g. Who can write the most outrageous hyperbole?)
- Make a newspaper
- Have a tea party to discuss a book

Before, During, and After Reading

SQ3R (Survey, Question, Read, Recite, Review)

This strategy is one of the most useful strategies for helping students organize text. It is especially useful for chapters in textbooks. See Bilmeyer, R., & Barton, M. L. (1998). Teaching Reading in the Content Areas for a complete guide to this strategy.

REAP (Read, Encode, Annotate, Ponder)

This process was conceptualized by Anthony Manzo (1994). For more information go to "Reap Central" at http://members.aol.com/ReadShop/REAP1. html.

The process is as follows:

R—Students read a selection.

E—Students encode (translate orally or in their minds) the message from the writer to their own words (paraphrase).

A—Students annotate what they have read by making notes to themselves about the text.

P—Students ponder what they have read by thinking about it, discussing it, letting others see what they have written about it.

Making a Book Come Alive

Jeffrey Whilhelm in his book, *You Gotta BE the Book*, explains several excellent strategies that can help struggling readers visualize a story. I especially love the SSR (Student Symbolic Response) strategy as follows (this is my adaptation):

Step 1: As students read, they make paper figures that represent the major characters in the story. (They may also do pictures of the setting.)

Step 2: Students make a "Reader Symbol" (It can be an eye or an animal, or anything to symbolize themselves as a reader).

Step 3: Students put their characters in a little box or baggie so that they will be available to act out scenes from the book.

Step 4: Students take turns acting out scenes in groups or in whole class discussions. I usually have to prompt them to talk about how the "Reader Symbol" is responding to what has been read.

Students may talk about the characters with which they are empathizing or how they are feeling about what is happening. In other words, how they are connecting with the story and creating meaning as they read.

This is a wonderful technique for making stories come alive for students at all levels of readiness. They all love this strategy.

Summary

These strategies are ways of making the primary source of content information more readable for students reading below grade level. They also help students who are at grade level. Advanced and gifted students definitely need access to enrichment materials. As a matter of fact, all students should have access to materials beyond the primary source of content information.

Finding Resources that go beyond the Textbook

In order to truly differentiate, you must find resources beyond your textbook. You have two options when it comes to developing content differentiation resources: buy them or find "free stuff."

Teachers are bombarded with catalogues of materials they can buy to help engage students. The Internet is literally bursting with Web sites from which teachers can find resources for sale and for free. Here are a few suggestions to help you find resources.

Search Engine Directories

Example: Google Directory–Reference > Education > Products and Services–K through 12. This directory is listed by order of quality, but can also be arranged alphabetically. The directory includes the Web address and a sentence about each company.

Education Resources

"Education Resources" has an annotated online directory of Web links and information resources that are helpful to teachers (http://www.ucp-utica.org/uwlinks/education.html).

School Media Center Resources

Never underestimate how many great materials are available for free from your media center or public library. Most librarians love to help teachers find resources to enhance classroom instruction. They are always willing to pull books and journals for book carts on any subject the teacher needs. Library sources go beyond hard copy books; most of them have excellent film libraries and large selections of magazines and journals.

Special Hard Copy Sources for Various Types of Readers

- ♦ "Picture Books" are great resources for teaching concepts to secondary students. Go to http://www.srv.net/~gale/older.html to find a wonderful list of "Picture Books for Older Readers."

  An excellent book worth investigating is *Worth a Thousand Words: An Annotated Guide to Picture Books for Older Readers.*

- ♦ The Graphic Novel is a relatively new genre that is making a big hit with all kinds of readers. Some of these "novels" cross over into the "comic book" genre; therefore, the lines are not exactly clear on what is a graphic novel and what is comic book. Nevertheless, these low-text, high-visual works are great resources for some reluctant readers. The following online sources of information may be accessed through www.google.com:

- www.my.voyager.net/~raiteri/graphicnovels.htm The author of this Web site is a librarian who has read extensively in this genre. The Web site also has a very long list of links to other Web sites for information on graphic novels and comics.

- www.graphicnovels.com This is a resource for buying graphic novels and comic books.

- www.geocities.com/SoHo/Study/4273/graphic.html This Web site has reviews of graphic novels by the Masked Bookwyrm (a.k.a. D. K. Latta); it seems to be a popular site, and may be hard to access. Two interesting articles: "What Teens Want: Thirty Graphic Novels You Can't Live Without" may be found in the *School Library Journal* (2002, August) and "Graphic Novels and the Curriculum Connection" in *Library Media Connection* (2003, November/December).

♦ Special needs programs also have book lists. This Web address, accessible through google.com offers great book lists that are related to the "Habits of Mind" (http://www.ascd.org/publications/book/2000costa1/2000costa1toc.html).

In addition, Amy Benjamin's book *Differentiated Instruction: A Guide for Middle and High School Teachers* contains 10 pages (pp. 56–65) of classic novels she recommends in order to differentiate instruction through independent reading,. She annotates the list according to these codes: Kiddie Lit Classic, Banned, Young Adult, and Play.

Patricia Phelan's book, *High Interest–Easy Reading: An Annotated Book list for Middle School and Senior High School* is an excellent resource for challenged readers.

Magazines and journals have great articles from which students can learn. Some of the best magazines for students are published by Scholastic. Go to www.scholastic.org for titles based on grade levels.

♦ Specialty catalogues have great resources for special learners (e.g., gifted and learning disabled). I recommend these catalogues for finding excellent education resources:

- For Gifted Students: Pieces of Learning, Royal Fireworks Press

- For Special Education: Globe Ferron, Celebration Press, Dale Seymour Publications, Good Year Books, and Modern Curriculum Press.

On-Line Resources

In this "Information Age," anyone who has access to the Internet can find resources that are engaging and informative for various learners. **Some helpful hints about searching for information follow:**

Excellent information about how to search the web for resources to differentiate content in your classroom is available in www.SearchEngineWatch.com by Danny Sullivan, Editor. Sullivan says you don't have to know anything fancy to do effective searches online. He says all you need to know are a few easy steps and concepts. He calls his steps, "Search Engine Math."

In "Search Engine Math" you need to know a few easy concepts. First, generally speaking, the more specific your search is, the more likely you will get what you want. You must tell the search engine exactly what you want. Sullivan uses this example: if you want information about Windows 98 bugs, you would not just type "Windows." You should type in exactly what your problem is: "I can't install a USB device in Windows 98," for example. This will often work best.

Sullivan says that to make sure you get all the pages with all the desired words, you should use the + (plus) symbol. For instance, with the example above, enter: +Windows +98 +bugs. If you want to find information about North Carolina, Tennessee, and Alabama, you would type +North Carolina +Tennessee +Alabama. Only pages that contain all three words would appear.

Another aspect of Search Engine Math is using the – (minus) symbol to delete words from your search. He says for example if you seek information on Bill Clinton, but you do not want information that included Monica Lewinsky, you would type clinton-lewinsky.

Another way to narrow a search is by using "(quotation marks) to multiply key words, meaning that if you wanted to find information on Windows 98 bugs, you might type "Windows 98 Bugs" Now only pages that have all the words in the exact order will appear in your search results.

You can also combine symbols such as "Bill Clinton"–"Monica Lewinsky" +"Hilary Clinton."

Sullivan insists that this Search Engine Math is good for about 90% of the searches a person would need to do; however, beyond those basic search strategies, you can refine and further control your searching by using a few helpful hints that can be found in his article "Power Searching for Anyone" accessible by going to www.SearchEngineWatch.com. Sullivan also has great rating charts and important information about the major search engines, directories, and crawlers, or spiders.

There are three main types of search engines: Search Crawler or Spider (Spyder), Directories, and Meta-Search engines.

The *Search Crawler* or *Spider* accesses a web site, reads it, and then follows links to other pages within the site. The spider is programmed to visit the site often to update the material. Whatever the Spider finds goes into the second part of the Search Engine, the index, which is like a database. When a researcher enters a keyword or words in the search box, the search engine searches its index to find those words and/or phrases and then reveals the matching results. Examples are Google (the most popular), AltaVista, and Excite

Directories are created by a person rather than by a robot or spider. Those who want their information posted in a directory submit their URL with a short description. Those that are accepted are posted in the directory. Directories can provide more targeted information. A search for the directory site looks for matches only within the descriptions submitted, not information found on web pages. Those wanting to update their information submit an online update to the webmaster of the directory. Examples of directories: Yahoo, AOL, and AltaVista.

Meta-search engines search other search engines. Examples are Ask.com, and Dogpile, Ask.com also has the distinction of being a search engine that allows questions in standard English syntax.

Go to http://www.cadenza.org/search_engine_terms/srchad.htm for an excellent glossary of search engine terms.

Internet Resources

Teachers can find excellent ideas online. Also having students use the Internet to locate their own differentiated materials is better than your having to look for those sources yourself. If you have access to a computer lab, you should make sure to use it for content differentiation. Reasons to use the Internet:

- ♦ Information is current,
- ♦ Topics are almost limitless,
- ♦ Presentation of information is more varied than that of hard copy resources,
- ♦ It allows students to do things traditional teaching materials cannot do, such as: take virtual field trips, communicate with interesting people from outside the school to gather information, get real time information, learn at their own pace, go off on tangents, and find information in a variety of languages

By the time students are in secondary school, most of them have fairly sophisticated searching skills; however, you may want to ensure that everyone has enough information to get a good start. When you make an assignment, make sure the each URL (Uniform Resource Locator) is current. It is extremely frustrating to search for places that no longer exist. And, make sure you have acceptable use documentation.

Here is a short list of interesting Web sites to get you started. It is best to do a search yourself to find exactly what you are looking for. The ideas are almost limitless.

The following is from "Web Sites to Help Teachers Create a More Challenging Curriculum for Gifted Students" by Jann H. Leppien, and "Interesting and Entertaining Internet Sites for Kids" by Del Siegle. Both articles appeared in *Teaching for High Potential*, Vol. II No. 2 September 2000, a publication of the National Association for Gifted Children, additional sources are from http://www.brittonkill.k12.ny.us/esweb/teacher/index.htm The Gateway to Educational Materials (GEM) is a project of the ERIC Clearinghouse on Information and Technology and the U.S. Department of Education. It is a tool for finding teaching materials on the Web.

Lesson Planning

Discovery Channel School (www.discoverychannelschool.com) has lesson plans, activities, virtual field trips, and more based on the Discovery Channel, the Learning Channel, Animal Planet, and the Travel Channel.

The Ask Eric Virtual Library (http://ericir.syr.edu) has posted over 1,100 interesting and unique lesson plans from teachers across the country. New lessons are added on a regular basis.

Columbia Education Center Lesson Plans (www.col-ed.org/cur) has plans for K–12 students. Teachers browse to find lessons pertaining to their subject area.

Searching for Information Online

Southwestern Bell Company (SBC) (http://www.kn.pacbell.com): This site is the Knowledge Network Explorer for SBC. It includes Blue Web'n and Filamentality and other search possibilities, including GEM (Gateway to Educational Materials). It has an excellent annotated list of learning sites.

Yahooligans (www.yahooligans.com) makes searching the web easy for kids. They can also play chess and other games in the games section.

KidsClick (http://sunsite.berkeley.edu/KidsClick!) is designed by librarians for students. When searching for information, students access sites and information written for kids.

Ask Jeeves for Kids (www. ajkids.com) is easy for kids to use and has a great section for "bored kids" and a "Magical Wizardry Tour."

General Curriculum

Awesome Library (www.awesomelibrary.org) contains information for parents, teachers, and students. It uses 14,000 reviewed resources and includes the top 5% used in education. It has a comprehensive and easy to use method of searching for resources.

Education World (www.education-world.com) has lesson plans in every subject area with regular updates on new education sites that are relevant based on the time of year.

Language Arts

The Young Author's Workshop (www.planet.eon.net/~bplarock/index.html) can be used for students in elementary and middle grades. This site walks students through writing and publishing. It also has links to Writer's Workshop and other creative writing sources.

CyberGuides (www.sdcoe.k12.ca.us/score/cyberguide.html) are units of instruction based on standards, linked to the Web, and based on important works of literature. Each "guide" has a student and teacher edition that includes a task, a process by which the task should be completed, and a rubric by which performance is assessed. This is an excellent source for differentiation because it provides teachers with multiple reading selections based on varied reading levels for each theme or topic.

The Children's Literature Web Guide (www.ucalgary.ca/~dkbrown) is a comprehensive resource for information about Internet resources related to books for children and young adults. It has links to authors on the Web, scripts for readers' theatre, ideas for teaching children's books, and resources for storytellers.

My Hero (http:///myhero.com/home.asp) is a Web site children and teens can visit to read about famous people like Mark Twain and Rosa Parks. The pictures and graphics are engaging, and accessing information is easy. Students can post what they write about their own heroes and see what other people have written about theirs.

Mathematics

Math Forum (http://forum.Swarthmore.edu): This Web site has a full range of information for K–12 to college and beyond. It is linked to Dr. Math and has a discussion group, web lessons and units, and problems of the week.

Geometry Center (www.geom.umn.edu) uses technology to help students visualize and communicate math and science concepts. It has Java technology, video animation, and software development sections.

MegaMathematics (www.c3.lanl.gov/mega-math) is an exciting Web site that helps students see the art of mathematics. It has hands-on activities that instruct and inspire students.

Figure This! (www.figurethis.org) has highly engaging and challenging problems that can be downloaded and used as homework for families and students.

Science

Hello Dolly: A WebQuest (http://www.powayschools.com/projects/dolly) is an excellent simulation about cloning. Students can participate as teams in an inquiry-based activity.

Science UTM (www.ScienceU.com) is a wonderful and comprehensive site. Where students can get information about science and can also design or create products based on knowledge of scientific concepts. This site is filled with interactive exhibits.

Gene School (http://library.thinkquest.org/28599) has a glossary of terms, a section on the history of genetics and an interactive section where students can participate in lab experiments.

Chem4kids.com (http://chem4kids.com/index.html) has basic information about biology, chemistry, physics, and physical geography.

The Environmental Education Network (http://www.envirolink.org/) is a Web site that encourages students to get involved to save the earth's resources. It has projects, games, puzzles, and experiments that inspire students.

How Stuff Works (www.howstuffworks.com) actually shows kids how things work. For instance, it shows how the gears in a car function.

Mad Scientists Network (www.madsci.org) has a section with information and web resources The MadSci Library, and it has Mad Labs, which has information about having fun with science.

Social Studies

The History Net (www.thehistorynet.com) makes history come alive for students with primary historical sources about every event imaginable. The site includes eyewitness accounts, interviews, and personality profiles of famous people.

History/Social Studies Web site for K–12 Teachers (http://execpc.com/~dboals/boals.html) helps teachers utilize the internet to differentiate instruction. Teachers can find a variety of resources for advanced learners.

Online Resources (http://socialstudies.com/online.html) has a wide variety of projects and activities including an Internet-based project based on elections. It has teacher-developed activities from the National Center for History in the Schools.

Social Studies Sources (http://edcuation.indiana.edu/~socialst) has the following categories: U.S. History and World History, diversity, general history, geography, and global studies.

The Arts

ArtsEdNet (www.getty.edu/artsnet/) has great lesson plans in the arts and a virtual exhibition of the art on the Web site and from other programs. This site helps art teachers and general classroom teachers use art in their curriculums. It is also of use to museum educators and teacher educators at the university level.

Music-Education Online (http://www.isd77.k12.mn.us/resources/staff pages/shirk/k12.music.html) has lesson plans and information about composers and musical instruments. It has excellent resources for music educators.

Connecting with Others

Classroom Connect (www.classroomconnect.com) has helpful information about opportunities for collaboration on Internet projects. This is the World Wide Web counterpart to the periodical, *Classroom Connect*. Includes GRADES (Global Resources and Directory of Educational Sites.)

Children's Express (www.cenews.org) was designed by children and provides a forum for students around the world to discuss monthly topics.

Kidlink (www.kidlink.org) encourages global dialogue for students up to age 15. It is supported by 38 public mailing lists and has a chat room. Volunteer teachers and parents provide input from around the world. The site can be accessed in 18 languages.

UNICEF Voices of Youth (www.unicef.org/voy) encourages students to voice their opinions on issues that affect children, such as child labor and children of war. It includes problems for students to solve.

Curiosity's FreeZone (www.freezone.com) is monitored by adults who remove any inappropriate responses. It includes pen pal lists and a bulletin board. Students can function as junior reporters to the site. This site if for students ages 10–16.

Interactive Sites

FunBrain (www.funbrain.com) has an abundance of activities, including a weekly current events quiz developed with specific age groups in mind. It is filled with interactive games.

Bonus (www.bonus.com) has great interactive activities for students. This is a highly interesting site for students of all ages and abilities.

Electronic Emissary Project (www.tapr.org/emissary) this site matches teachers' classrooms with experts in various fields.

Miscellaneous Educational Sites

B.J. Homework Helper (www. bjpinchbeck.com) is a popular Web site developed by B.J., a 13 year old who lives in New Brighton, Pennsylvania. He helps with homework, research, and if a kid needs something, B.J. probably has it.

Northwestern University (www.nwu.eud/world/desk-reference.html) has links to online resources that are helpful to kids, such as dictionaries, thesauruses and other reference materials.

Exposure (www.88.com/exposure/lowrez_i.htm) explains the concepts of modern photography. It is appealing to all ages.

First Family Pets, Socks and Buddy (www.whitehouse.gov/kids/) helps kids learn about children and pets who lived in the white house. And much more!

4teachers: Teachers can use this Web site to post assignments that students and their parents can access. Teachers can set up the assignments by going to www.4teachers.org, and then clicking on the "Assign-A-Day" section for teachers. The site will walk you through setting up an assignment and how students and parents can do a student calendar search to access the assignment.

Online Projects

International E-mail Classroom Connections-IECC-Projects (www.iecc.org) explains many online projects and has a place where teachers and students can request help on projects, surveys and questionnaires.

International Education and Resource Network-IEARN (www.iearn.org) has projects in which students all over the world can participate so that they can make contributions to saving the resources of our planet. IEARN has projects teachers can access in the following: language arts, science, and social studies.

Education Place (www.eduplace.com/index.html) has several activities sponsored by Houghton-Mifflin. It has easily accessed tele-collaboration projects.

KIDLINK/KIDPRO (www.kidlink.org/KIDPROJ) has a list of projects for children in over 103 countries.

Filamentality Online Support (www.kn.pacbell.com/wired/fil): This site sponsored by Pacific Bell let students create their own Web sites without needing to know html. There are example sites to explore in this exciting Web site.

The WebQuest Page (http://edweb.sdsu.edu/webquest/webquest.html) focuses on inquiry-based learning activities that conserve students' time because they are about using information rather than searching for it. It has rubrics for evaluating the quality of the WebQuest and other teacher and student resources.

Special Internet Resources

Beyond the typical use of the Internet in the classroom, here are a few especially interesting uses of the Internet.

MUD and MOO

A MUD is a Multiple User Domain/Dungeon or Dialogue computer program that allows users to adopt a persona in order to walk around and chat with other personas a specially designed space (http://www.mudconnect.com/ mudfaq/mudfq-p1.html). Users can solve puzzles and fight battles with monsters and other personas, and create their own spaces, descriptors and props. Go to http://www.mudconnect.com to find a mud.

Learn about using a MOO (Multiple User Domain Object Oriented) to teach. A MOO is a text-based virtual environment, like a chat room with an architecture of interconnected rooms, characters, and objects that can be manipulated. MOO players can create, describe, and program aspects of the MOO environment.

See Robert Adams Rozema's article in *The English Journal,* Vol. 93, No.1, September 2003, to read about his exciting use of a literary MOO. Go to LogMOO for further information.

MUDs and MOOs are considered games; therefore some schools may not allow students to access them.

BLOG

Also check how you might use a BLOG in your classroom. A BLOG is part Web site and part journal entry or log of what is happening in a person's life. BLOGs are potentially highly informative and each one is unique in style and content. For information about how to get connected with the art of blogging, go to http://www.smilezone.com/blogs/basics.htm

Organizing Materials

Finally, now that you know how to create materials or to find a wide range of materials to differentiate your content, here are a few suggestions about how to organize the materials:

1. **Theme Baskets**: Theme baskets can be used in two basic ways: using various theme baskets to support several learning circle groups or using

one basket to support a whole class unit of study. If you are heterogeneously grouping students, suggested contents related to the stated theme might be:

- a picture book,

- a children's chapter book,

- enough copies for each group member to have the core selection,

- one copy of an advanced reading selection,

- one copy of a nonfiction selection that is related to the theme.

Teachers might require students to read the core selection and one or two other pieces of information in the basket.

Alternative: If you want to tier the baskets, try including the resources based on students grouped by readiness, interests, or learning styles. Each basket could have resources that relate to the same theme or topic; however,

- For readiness differentiation you could have a low, medium, and high basket of materials.

- For interests differentiation you could make baskets that capture the interests of most of your students, such as a sports basket, an arts basket, and a social basket.

- For learning styles differentiation you could have baskets based on the some or all of the Multiple Intelligences.

Baskets can be a festive way to hold materials; however, tubs or boxes or any large enough resources could be used to organize differentiated materials.

From Richison, Jeannine D., Hernandez, Anita C., and Carter, Marcia. "Blending Multiple Genres in Theme Baskets," *The English Journal.* November, 2002.

2. **Learning or Enrichment Centers**: An interesting way to organize and present differentiated content materials and resources is in a Learning or Enrichment Center. An easy way to make a center is to use a science project tri-fold presentation board, or any other method of organizing differentiated content materials that gets students' interest. If the shape of the center matches the information, students will be extremely curious and want to explore. For instance, a learning center about caves could be designed to look like a cave or a history center on weapons of war could look like a small fort.

3. **Task Cards:** Another way to organize and present differentiated content materials is by using task cards [see Kaplan, Gould, and Siegel, (1995) for

an example of using task cards to differentiate instruction for gifted students]. You could develop cards that direct students to examine specific materials and resources or to go online to find these resources. The cards can be organized by simply placing them in envelopes or they could be organized on a bulletin board or as a book of choices.

4. **Tubs**: Find colorful or clear plastic tubs in which to place materials. Tubs can be labeled and indexed so that students can keep them in order. Assignments can be taped to the outside of the tub or placed in the tub.

5. **Cubing**: Make 6-sided cubes that have different assignments or questions listed on them. Students turn the cubes to determine which assignment or question they should answer orally, or in written form. You may use one cube for each unit or use several cubes based on different models of instruction. For instance you could have a cube with assignments for each of Gardner's (1993) "Multiple Intelligences" or you could have a cube that has questions that represent each of Wiggins', Grant, and McTighe's 91998) "facets of understanding." See Chapter 3 for more on this technique.

6. **Envelopes or folders**: Use large envelopes or folders to organize problems, assignments, questions, and resources for tiered lessons. Younger students are engaged by interesting methods of organizing material; however, for high school students, you can probably get away with simply placing tiered assignments in folders or envelopes that are clearly labeled and that include assignments with accopanying materials.

Summary

Too often teachers feel limited by their textbooks, which in most cases are written for on-grade level students; however, because all students are not on grade level, teachers must find resources to differentiate their materials so that all students may learn to access information through print. Options for below grade level students include making the textbook readable by using scaffolding strategies or finding alternative texts for them. Options for above grade level students include enriching their learning by finding more challenging materials for them or having them find their own resources. Textbooks also have limited appeal in terms of students' interests; therefore, teachers should be able to turn to technology resources to improve the interest level in their content areas. In terms of learning styles and preferences, teachers need to gather resources, and they need to learn about techniques that address all learners. Access to the Internet has made it possible to find almost anything you need to find. We are, as we all know, in the midst of *The Information Age*.

3

Selecting a Process

Depending on the personalities and interests of the students in your classes, the mix of readiness levels of those students, and the units you are planning to teach them, you may choose one of three differentiation processes: whole class, small group, or individual student differentiation. Several methods are described for each category and provide a least one example from a variety of secondary subject areas.

Whole Class Differentiation

Whole class differentiation is about looking at the entire class and differentiating instruction by putting students into groups or by employing other methods that allow all students in the class to work at their individual levels of readiness, learning styles, or interests. You would most likely choose whole class differentiation if you had at least two or three distinct levels of readiness in the class.

Tiered Lessons

Developing tiered lessons for heterogeneously grouped classes takes some time, but the results allow all of your students to be challenged at their own specific readiness level, and permit you to more closely match their learning styles and interests. You can tier a lesson for two or more levels of students' readiness. Most teachers have a sense of low, middle, and high readiness levels in a heterogeneously grouped class; therefore it is reasonable to design a lesson for those three levels.

It is important to remember that you should be teaching the *same objectives* to all students, and mastery of the content should take *the same amount of time*. For instance, high level students should not be given *more* projects than lower students; however, they can read faster so they could be given more to read. Most importantly, even though the level of difficulty will be different for each tier, each student should be *challenged* to do his/her best at whatever level he/she is performing.

For students who are struggling with a topic (Level 1), you would want to give them an assignment that has the following features:

- Requires less difficult independent reading.
- Has materials based on the average reading level of the participants, which is usually below grade level.
- Has spare text and lots of graphic aids.
- Has a low level of abstraction, i.e., as concrete as possible.
- Requires fewer steps to complete the assignment
- Converges on "right answers" to solve problems.
- Requires only knowledge and comprehension levels of thinking for independent work.
- Includes supportive strategies, such as graphic organizers or teacher prompting to help students infer and draw conclusions. (i.e., use higher level thinking skills)

For average learners (Level 2), the assignment should include the following features:

- Includes independent reading materials from the textbook or other on-grade level sources.
- Uses concrete concepts to help students transition to more abstract concepts.
- Includes questions or problems that are a mix of open-ended and "right answers."
- Can have more steps.
- Expects students to infer and draw conclusions with less teacher support. Teacher should count on being on hand if necessary to prompt students in this area.
- Ensures that students can be successful with knowledge, comprehension, and application on their own, and that with help they can address some of the high levels of thinking.

For advanced or gifted learners (Level 3), the assignment should include the following features:

- Includes reading materials from sources more complex than the textbook, if possible.
- Requires more lengthy sources because students can read faster than lower or average students.
- Focuses on abstract concepts as much as possible and uses open-ended questions exclusively.
- Requires students to infer and evaluate.
- Assumes students have knowledge, comprehension, and application abilities, and that they will be challenged only if you ask them to analyze, synthesize, and evaluate.

Example: Computer Technology:
Writing a Report and Building a Data Base

Objective: Students will use keyboarding and a data base to present information that is integrated with Social Studies.

Level 1	Level 2	Level 3
Assessments: 1. A **report** on the animal Criteria: ♦ two pages of text Works cited correctly ♦ 10 note cards ♦ Accurate information ♦ Three sources of information ♦ Pictures (optional) ♦ Cover sheet neat and creative ♦ Double-spaced Neat and organized ♦ Correct form for expository report 2. A **database** comparing an animal that lives in a specific country with other animals that live in that country	Assessments: 1. A **report** on a country Criteria: ♦ three pages of text ♦ Works cited correctly ♦ 14 note cards ♦ Accurate information ♦ three sources of information ♦ Pictures (optional) ♦ Cover sheet neat and creative ♦ Double-spaced ♦ Neat and organized ♦ Correct form for expository report 2. A **database** comparing a country in a region to at least four other countries in the region	Assessments: 1. A **report** on a topic Criteria: ♦ 5 pages of text ♦ Works cited correctly 25 note cards ♦ Accurate information ♦ three sources of information. ♦ Pictures (optional) ♦ Cover sheet neat and creative ♦ Double-spaced ♦ Neat and organized ♦ Correct form for expository report 2. A **database** that supports the proof of the thesis statement

Criteria:

♦ Database must include five points of comparison on five animals.

♦ Information must be complete and accurate.

Materials:

♦ Computers for keyboarding, developing a database, and researching.

♦ Note cards

♦ Hard copy books and articles of animals from countries of study

♦ A syllabus (see examples) for students.

♦ Markers or crayons for artwork

Activities:

♦ Step1: Hand out syllabus and go over requirements.

♦ Step 2: Teach computer research skills.

♦ Step 3: Teach or review note-taking skills and citing sources.

♦ Step 4: Students use computers and hard copy materials to take notes and cite sources.

♦ Step 4: Teach data base development.

♦ Step 5: Students put data they have found into databases.

♦ Step 6: Teach or review organizing note cards to develop a report. (See "Research Paper Syllabus" on page 127 of this chapter for details.)

♦ Step 7: Students write and revise reports.

♦ Step 8: Students present their work to the teacher and to the class.

Level 1 Syllabus

Find information in order to compose a typed report (2 pages) on an animal from a country in the continent you are studying.

1. Choose an animal.
2. Find the following information:
   - Class—mammal, amphibian, reptile, etc.
   - Habitat—where the animal is found (i.e., what countries)
   - Habitat—type of living environment (i.e., cave, web, underwater, nest, etc.)
   - Food—what the animal eats
   - Food—how the animal eats
   - Average weight
   - Color
   - Interesting physical features
   - Interesting habits
   - Natural enemies
3. For each of the above categories, you should have **at least one "note"** about that topic copied from a book or an electronic resource. Your notes may either be on index cards or on pieces of notebook paper. Your notes will be turned in with the report. **You need a minimum of 10 notes to write your report.**
4. You should use at least three resources (books, magazines, encyclopedias, the Internet, etc.) to find information on your topic. You should also make a **bibliography note** for each resource. You need to be able to show clearly where you got your information. The bibliography note includes the following and in this order (ask the media specialist if your source is

missing any of these parts): Book's author (last name first). Title of the book or article. Place published: Publisher, date published.

Notice: See that the bibliography note is written with hanging indentation and put each punctuation mark as written above. **Do not make up your own form**.

5. You should make a **Works Cited** page at the end of your report to show from where all your information came.

6. Handwrite a report that has an introduction, body, and conclusion. You will use keyboarding skills to type the report in keyboarding class.

7. Build a database as part of your report. Compare your animal to at least four other animals in terms of at least five of these possible categories:
   - Type of the animal
   - Class—mammal, amphibian, reptile, etc.
   - Habitat—where the animal is found (i.e., what countries)
   - Habitat—type of living environment (i.e., cave, web, underwater, nest, etc.)
   - Food—what the animal eats
   - Food—how the animal eats
   - Average weight
   - Color
   - Interesting physical features
   - Interesting habits
   - Natural enemies

Level 2 Syllabus

Find information in order to compose a typed report (three pages) on one of the countries of a continent you are studying.

1. Choose a country from a region in the continent you have chosen.

2. Find the following types of information:
   - history of the country
   - population groups (racial, ethnic, religious)
   - important leaders from the country
   - arts and literature from the country
   - main points of interest in the country
   - the capital and other major cities
   - other interesting information about the country

3. For each of the above categories, you should have **at least two "notes"** about that topic copied from a book or an electronic resource. Your notes may either be on index cards or on pieces of notebook paper. Your notes will be turned in with the report. **You need a minimum of 14 notes to write your report.**

4. You should use at least three resources (books, magazines, the Internet, etc., **no encyclopedias!**) to gather information for your report. You should also make a **bibliography note** for each resource. You need to be able to show clearly where you got your information. The bibliography note includes the following and in this order (ask the media specialist if your source is missing any of these parts): Book's author (last name first). Title of the book or article. Place published: Publisher, date published.

   Notice: See that the bibliography note is written with hanging indentation and place each punctuation mark as written above. **Do not make up your own form**.

5. You should make a **Works Cited** page at the end of your report to show from where all your information came.

6. Handwrite a report that has an introduction, body, and conclusion. You will use keyboarding skills to type the report in keyboarding class.

7. Attach a printed data base to your report that compares your country to at least four other countries in the same region. Include at least five of these categories of information in the data base:
   - name of the country
   - longitude
   - latitude
   - population groups
   - population
   - chief lakes
   - chief rivers
   - chief mountain ranges and peaks
   - chief deserts
   - gross national product
   - highest geographical point
   - lowest geographical point
   - bordering countries
   - major exports
   - major industries
   - major products

- type of government
- capital
- date it became a country
- other interesting information about the country that distinguishes it.

Level 3 Syllabus

Find information in order to compose a typed report (5 pages) on a topic of interest in your Social Studies curriculum.

1. Choose a topic and write a thesis statement that can be proved.
2. Find information on your topic that helps you prove your thesis statement.
3. You should have **at least 25 "notes"** about that topic copied from a book or an electronic resource. Your notes may either be on index cards or on pieces of notebook paper. Your notes will be turned in with the report. **You need a minimum of 25 notes to write your report.**
4. You should use at least three resources (books, magazines, the Internet, etc., **no encyclopedias!**) to gather information for your report. You should also make a **bibliography note** for each resource. You need to be able to show clearly where you got your information. The bibliography note includes the following and in this order (ask the media specialist if your source is missing any of these parts): Book's author (last name first). Title of the book or article. Place published: Publisher, date published.

   Notice: See that the bibliography note is written with hanging indentation and put each punctuation mark as written above. **Do not make up your own form**.

5. You should make a **Works Cited** page at the end of your report to show from where all your information came.
6. Handwrite a report that has an introduction, body, and conclusion. You will use keyboarding skills to type the report in keyboarding class.
7. You must develop a data base that helps prove your thesis statement.

4Mat

This type of lesson attempts to address all learning styles (see Chapter 1 for more detail). Lessons are divided into eight steps that address learning needs that are random and sequential, and concrete and abstract in various combinations.

Lesson Tiered by Learning Styles (Multiple Intelligences and Visual, Auditory, Kinesthetic/Haptic)

Note that whenever you attempt to differentiate for learning styles, you need to be able to accommodate more sound and movement going on together in the room. If your classroom cannot accommodate multifaceted activities, you may need to find another space (like your media center) or find a way to segment your space. Some schools permit teachers to allow students to work in the halls outside the classroom and some do not. With differentiation for learning styles, you do need to be able to spread out enough so that students' activities do not interfere with each other.

Template for Unit Tiered by Learning Styles

Unit Theme:					
Topic:					
Goals:					
Objectives:					
Acceptable Evidence of mastery:					
Whole Class Engagement:					
Activities Differentiated by Multiple Intelligences (such as):					
Verbal/ Linguistic	Logical/ Mathematical	Kinesthetic	Spatial	Musical	Naturalist
OR					
Visual		Auditory		Kinestheic/Haptic	

Example of a Social Studies Tiered Unit
Based on Multiple Intelligences

Students should use extra class time in Social Studies class and time at home to work independently (intrapersonal) or with a partner (interpersonal) on this project.

1. Choose a country (or a tribe) from a specific region in Africa.

2. Choose **one activity for each of the five organizing questions** (i.e., You should have five distinct parts). As you develop your chosen activity make sure you **answer all of the sub-categories** associated with the organizing questions. If part of your project requires a class presentation, you must arrange to get a few minutes of class time to present.

Question I: Who are the people of your African country and what are their beliefs and values?

A. Explain what the people of your country look like.

B. Explain what a typical family is like. Discuss their values, beliefs, customs, and traditions.

C. Explain the kinds of art (drama, literature, visual arts, music, dance, etc.) they produce?

Question II: What is the environment in which the people of your African country live?

A. Describe the absolute and relative location of the country and include the absolute and relative locations of major land forms, bodies of water, and natural resources.

B. Explain how the geography of the country affects the people (e.g., where they live, what they do, how they adapt).

C. Evaluate the effectiveness of the people's use of the land.

Question III: How is the society in your African country organized?

A. Explain the history of government in your country. (That is: How has the government changed over time?)

B. Explain how the government is currently organized in your country? (Include the following: how leaders are elected, how branches of government work, how laws are made.)

C. Evaluate your country's interaction with other countries of the world.

D. Evaluate the method of government in your African country. Does it promote justice? Explain.

Question IV: How do people in your African country make a living?

A. Identify resources found in your African country and explain the relationship between the location of the resources and the jobs that are available.

B. Are the resources equally distributed in your country? Explain how the distribution of resources affects the people.

C. Evaluate the influence of inventions, discoveries, and innovations on the economic development of your country.

D. Judge how changes in the movement of people, goods, and ideas have affected ways of living for the people of your country.

E. Explain the economic relationships your country has with other countries of the world.

F. Explain how health issues have affected the economy of your country.

Question V: How has the society of your country changed over time?

A. Identify people, symbols, and events associated with the heritage of the people of your country.

B. Discuss changes that have occurred in ways of living in your country and judge the effect of these changes on the lives of the people.

C. Explain how the people of your country transmitted their values, beliefs, and customs.

All work will be evaluated using the "Product Guide" (a list of requirements for each product choice).

Author note: You may do a **"report"** on each of these questions or you may choose activities/products from the "Multiple Intelligence Matrix."

Multiple Intelligence Matrix

Intelligence	Question 1	Question 2
Linguistic	Create a skit about an African family. Use puppets to act it out.	Make a flyer advertising the beauty of your country.
Logical/Math	Create a database to show the data you collect about the people of your country.	Design charts and graphs to show the data about the environment of your country.
Spatial	Make a poster, a model village, a picture book, or a pop-up book about the people of your country.	Draw maps, use diagrams, or make a relief map to show the geography of your country.
Kinesthetic	Write a skit and act it out or do a symbolic dance about the people of your country. Write a brief interpretation of the dance.	Use props that represent geographical aspects of your country. Show with movement how they fit together.
Musical	Find a song or music from your country. Write a brief explanation of how the music reflects the values and traditions of the people.	Create music that symbolizes the land forms and environment of your country. Write a brief explanation of how the music is symbolic.
Naturalist	Choose any of the above methods to show the people in their environment of your country.	Choose any of the above methods. Focus on the affects of people on the environment of your country.

Question 3	Question 4	Question 5
Make up a speech you might give if you were trying to be elected president of your country.	Write a letter to an imaginary pen pal encouraging or discouraging him/her to come to your country to find a job.	Write a folktale a griot would tell about the history of your country.
Use graphic organizers to address the way society is organized in your country.	Use graphs to show the information you gather about the economy in your country.	Do a timeline of the history of your country.
Make a multi-medium collage that reflects the government of your country.	Create a diorama showing the way the people earn a living in your country.	Make a pictorial time line of the history of your country.
Create a video or do this live: Write a talk show in which you interview a leader or leaders of your country about their government.	Design a documentary or music video to address the economy of your country.	Dress up as a person from your country. Tell a brief history of your country.
Write a ballad about the government of your country. Include the issue of justice.	Design at least two commercial jingles advertising your country.	Find at least 2 songs that relate to the history of your country. Write why these songs are relevant to the country's history.
Choose any of the above methods. Focus on the government's affect on the environment of your country.	Choose any of the above methods. Focus on the economy's affect on the environment of your country.	Choose any of the above methods. Focus on the history of how the people protect or do not protect the environment of their country.

Here is an example of **Differentiated Prompts Based on the Four Learning Styles** (Silver, Strong, and Perini, 2000; see Chapter 1).

The Civil War

Mastery Style: Make a graphic organizer that shows the reasons given by the South and the North for fighting the Civil War.	Self-Expression Style: Get a partner and role-play a conversation between a Southern soldier and a Northern soldier.
Understanding Style: Explain what the Civil War meant to our country as part of our cultural heritage.	Interpersonal Style: Imagine you are a soldier on either side of the Civil war. Find a way to present your feelings about the war to the class or in a small group.

The following table graphically demonstrates how Silver, Strong, and Perini might connect the ideas of Learning Styles with the Multiple Intelligences. Some possible generic assignments related to a topic of study for each of the core subjects could be:

English—the critical analysis of a novel, short story, nonfiction work, poem

Math—word problems that require a number of mathematical processes to solve

Social Studies—an historical event or social issue

Science—scientific concepts or phenomena.

4 Learning Styles and the Multiple Intelligences

Mastery Style	Understanding Style	Self-Expression Style	Interpersonal Style
Multiple Intelligence: Verbal			
♦ Write lists of concepts or information related to a topic of study. ♦ Explain the steps to solve a problem from a topic of study. ♦ Take a multiple choice test on something read in a topic of study.	♦ Write to an argumentative prompt. ♦ Analyze the meaning of something read. ♦ Take an open-ended essay test on the information from a topic of study.	♦ Get into a group and discuss (and record) answers. ♦ Write a script and role-play. ♦ Write a poem showing how you relate to a person or community in what you have read.	♦ Write a creative story about something you have read. ♦ Find a way to show orally or in writing your insights about a topic about which you have read.
Multiple Intelligence: Logical/Mathematical			
♦ Construct a graphic organizer showing the relationships of ideas. ♦ Determine the percentages or other mathematical concepts that emerge from a topic. ♦ Find the solution to a math problem by taking the correct steps.	♦ Explain why certain operations are necessary to solve a mathematical problem. ♦ Conduct an investigation and construct a database to explain the meaning of phenomena. ♦ Do research and compile data about a topic of study.	♦ Show how mathematical concepts are important in activities related to a topic of study. ♦ Make a budget for a shopping spree or for a special meal for your family.	♦ Create a graphic organizer or other mathematical solution to solve a problem. ♦ Find a way to show mathematically how two topics are related to each other in an unusual way.
Multiple Intelligence: Spatial			
♦ Draw a picture of an important aspect of a topic to address specific guidelines. ♦ Build a 5" model to address a specific problem. Find the errors.	♦ Draw a picture or construct a model that symbolizes the meaning of something about which you have read or experienced.	♦ Work in a group to make a collage that represents the feelings experienced by the people in a story or in a real world problem.	♦ Find a creative way to draw or build a representation of the issues associated with a specific problem related to a topic of study.

Mastery Style	Understanding Style	Self-Expression Style	Interpersonal Style
Multiple Intelligence: Musical			
◆ Find five songs that are examples of something related to a topic. ◆ Make up a ballad with six stanzas that tell about a topic of study.	◆ Write a song or find a song that explains the meaning of an issue in a topic of study. ◆ Write a song that symbolizes a concept from a topic of study.	◆ Find at least five songs that represent the way people view or respond to a topic. (Work with a partner or in a small group.) ◆ Explain how music is important to the study of a topic.	◆ Create a musical product that solves a problem in a topic of study.
Multiple Intelligence: Bodily/ Kinesthetic			
◆ Make up a movement that includes five movements related to a topic of study. ◆ Develop a movement that helps you remember important facts about a topic of study.	◆ Choreograph a dance that symbolically represents your interpretation of a theme in a topic of study.	◆ Work with a partner or in a group to role play an example of an important issue in a topic of study. ◆ Work with a partner or in a small group to design a pantomime that shows an important social problem and how to solve it.	◆ Create a movement or dance that displays your understanding of the concepts of a unit of study.
Multiple Intelligence: Interpersonal			
◆ Organize a team to develop a set of directions to accomplish a specific task within a topic of study.	◆ Organize a research team to find the answers to issues presented in a topic of study.	◆ Divide the roles in your group to solve a problem that is related to a topic of study.	◆ Find a method for the group to solve a problem related to a unit of study.

Mastery Style	Understanding Style	Self-Expression Style	Interpersonal Style
Multiple Intelligence: Intrapersonal			
♦ Write a journal response to a topic of study. Include your feelings about an issue related to that topic. Self-assess your response to a test of your knowledge of a topic.	♦ Self-evaluate your interpretation of the events or actions related to a topic of study.	♦ Explain how you personally respond to a problem or issue that effects our society.	♦ Find a way to show how you use your knowledge of yourself to solve a problem in a topic of study.
Multiple Intelligence: Naturalist			
♦ Make a graphic organizer or list of issues that show how a topic of study is related to the natural world.	♦ Interpret how a topic of study is related to the ecology of our planet.	♦ Work with a group to explore through nature how to solve a specific problem within a topic of study.	♦ Create a method using the forces of nature to deal with a problem within a topic of study.

Using Interest Groups to Differentiate Instruction

Although this differentiation strategy focuses on students' interests, it can also be leveled so that student readiness is a consideration. Activities should be designed so that students may work independently. They may also be used for enrichment for students who have mastered objectives more quickly than others. This strategy allows students to deepen their knowledge of topics in which they are interested. Groups can be developed from the assessment of students' interests at the beginning of the year. There are several types of study groups as the following: issues discussion, book discussion, topic-centered discussion, research, and writing.

A Template for Designing Interest Groups

Unit of Study:				
Theme:				
Interest Groups:				
Group #1	Group #2	Group #3	Group #4	Group #5
Materials: Activities: Product:	Materials: Activities: Product:	Materials: Activities: Product:	Materials: Activities: Product:	Materials: Activities: Product:

Example of Interest Groups Strategy

If a math teacher analyzed her math class and realized she had students with four distinct interests, she could use "Interest Groups" to help her students understand concepts with which they might be having trouble. Most likely some of the students would fit in more than one category; therefore, she should let them choose their strongest interest. She should also let students choose their groups; however, she should ask them to help keep the groups balanced and require that they avoid being in a "friends" group. Here is an example helping students learn more about "Ratios and Proportions" using students' interests to make these somewhat abstract ideas more concrete for them.

Unit of Study: Ratios and Proportions			
Theme: How are ratios and proportions used in real world situations and/or to solve real world problems?			
Interest Groups: All groups will answer this question in a presentation to the class. How did you use ratios and proportions in real world situations and/or to solve a real world problem within your topic of interest? Groups will make a creative presentation to the class that will include the following: a visual (such as a chart or picture), a shared oral presentation, and an individual written report explaining what you learned from the interest group experience about ratios and proportions. The presentation will be evaluated by check sheet.			
Group1: Sports Fans	Group 2: Shoppers	Group 3: Music Lovers	Group 4: Visual Artists

Materials:

- Textbooks
- Computers
- Articles found in journals, magazines, encyclopedias or online
- Markers, cards, poster board, glue

Activities:

1. As a whole class, discuss how to begin the inquiry process (especially how to divide the topic)
2. Group work: Begin the inquiry by allowing students the opportunity to find a variety of sources about their area of interest in the media center, the computer lab, and at home.
3. Read materials, discuss ideas, and take notes.
4. Share results of inquiry and discuss how to answer the question and present information to the class.

   Author note: The teacher should float from group to group answering questions, making suggestions, and directing students toward solid mathematical solutions. The teacher should correct any wrong directions or inaccurate math work.

5. Divide tasks and create the various elements of the assignment.
6. Present to class.

Product: See Syllabus with "check sheet" evaluation.

Syllabus for Ratios and Proportions Interest Groups

Process:

1. Choose one of the following interest groups: Sports Fans, Shoppers, Music Lovers, or Visual Artists.
2. Within your interest group, discuss how to begin the inquiry process in order to answer this question: How are ratios and proportions used in real world situations and/or to solve real world problems?
3. Inquiry: Find a variety of sources within your interest area in the media center, computer lab, and at home.
4. Read materials and take notes.
5. Share results of inquiry and discuss how to answer the question and present information to the class.
6. Divide the tasks and create the various elements of the assignment.
7. Present to the class.

Products:

Each group must develop the following products:

1. A visual that demonstrates the following elements:
   - accuracy of information
   - sufficiency of information
   - neatness
   - creativity
   - artistic design

2. A group oral presentation taken from note cards. The presentation must include the following elements:

   ♦ accurate information

   ♦ sufficient information

   ♦ audible information

   ♦ important role taken by each member of the group

   ♦ creativity

3. An individual written report explaining what you learned about ratios and proportions from participating in the interest group experience.

   ♦ sufficient evidence of learning

   ♦ accurate information

   ♦ detailed examples

   ♦ significant conclusions drawn about real world connections

Grading

Visual	=	20 points (4 points per check)	Report	=	40 points (10 points per check)
Presentation	=	40 points (8 points per check)	Total		100 points

Groups will rate each member to determine that individual's involvement in the study group using the list below.

List each member of the group. Rate his/her involvement in developing the products:

Name: _____   Grade: _____

            _____   _____

            _____   _____

            _____   _____

            _____   _____

            _____   _____

The overall grade will be a combination of points earned and the average of the grades determined by fellow group members.

Learning Centers

A learning center can be a creatively designed "place" a student goes to to work mostly independently on an assignment that can be placed in a folder or other organized method within the center. Learning centers can be differentiated for interests, readiness, and learning styles.

How to Set up a Learning Center or Centers in the Classroom

♦ Step 1: Decide what unit you want to teach and why centers would be the best method of teaching the themes, goals, and objectives of that topic.

♦ Step 2: Find a place or places to set up the centers.

♦ Step 3: Identify materials you will need to develop the centers such as the following:

- Tables and chairs
- Computers
- Tri-fold or bi-fold cardboard display boards (those sold for Science Fair projects work well).
- Televisions
- VCR or DVD
- Sets of boxes or book shelves
- Bean bag chairs, folding chairs, or rugs
- Lamps
- Bulletin boards
- Carts
- Clothes lines and clothes pins (for hanging assignments)
- Any kind of high tech or interesting materials available for hands-on exploration.

Author note: Students are engaged by creativity; therefore if the center looks like the subject of study, students can be truly hooked into visiting that center.

Ideas

- A study of pirates could have a treasure chest, a pirate simulated ship hull (or picture of one on cardboard), a cardboard closet, or rack for hanging pirate clothes, etc.
- A study of the planets could have a cardboard space ship control room or other simulations of a space ship, a mobile of planets, a simulation of a planet surface, etc.

- A study of any war could have an old chest with artifacts from that war, a war games board with toy soldiers, a table with battle planning maps, an old radio or simulation of one with tapes that simulate or chronicle an event or events of the war, etc.

- A study of Shakespeare (or one of his plays) could include a simulation of the Globe theater, a clothes rack for costumes, a table of paper dolls or stuffed or plastic dolls or puppets for dressing them in authentic costumes and/or acting scenes, a puppet theater, an old table and ink for composing in a 16th century looking environment.

◆ Step 4: Gather resources and write task assignments for each center. Make sure to include a list of the materials in the center and check them after each use to make sure you have them all. Make sure tasks require students to produce an assessable product to heighten accountability.

◆ Step 5: Orient students to the center or centers. Tell students the following:

  - How long they may stay in the center or centers.

  - If they will be in the center by themselves, with a partner, or as a small group.

  - What they are expected to turn in each time they are in a center or centers.

  - The condition in which they are to leave the center (i.e., with all materials in tact).

  - The order in which they may visit a center or centers (i.e., how they will take turns).

Learning Center Design Template

Unit of Study:

Theme:

Learning Centers:

Center #1	Center #2	Center #3	Center #4	Center #5
Materials:	Materials:	Materials:	Materials:	Materials:
Activities:	Activities:	Activities:	Activities:	Activities:
Product:	Product:	Product:	Product:	Product:

Example of a Lesson Using Learning Centers

Unit of Study: Students will study a country of their choice in order to prove that the cultural diversity represented by the country is worth preserving.

Theme: Cultural Diversity

Learning Centers:

♦ Students will choose a country in any region or a region determined by the teacher. They will gather resources about that country, such as a textbook or other hard copy source and an Internet source.

♦ Students will bring the information they have gathered about their country to each learning center.

♦ Students will spend a maximum or 45 minutes per class period for approximately 10 class periods. (This time could be adjusted based on ability of the class.)

♦ Students will visit centers individually, with a partner or in a group of no more than 4 students (teacher decides).

♦ Students will turn in completed work from their visits to the center.

♦ Students will leave the center as they found it.

♦ Students will take turns rotating through each center. They will visit each center a minimum of two times. The teacher should be able to store incomplete work between visits.

Center#1:	**Map Making Materials:** Center will be a table with a bifold or trifold poster of a map as a model. Poster board Paint Markers Pens Modeling clay or other substance for making a physical map (optional). **Task:** Create a map of your country so that you can explain how its geography is related to its culture. **Product:** A physical or other map of the country.
Center#2:	**Data Base Materials:** Center will be a computer(s) station. Computer Paper **Task:** Make a data base that includes at least the following categories: Race Language Economy Politics Religions Healthcare, so that you can show how the demographics might affect the cultural diversity. **Product:** A data base that is accurate and comprehensive.
Center #3:	**Religion/Traditions Materials:** Center will be a trunk of materials and a table. Cloth Pins Ropes/sashes Posterboard Paint Pens Markers Beads Glitter String Clay Small boxes Magazines **Task:** Create a visual that reflects the religious or other traditions of the country. The visual should show the aesthetic and humanistic elements of the culture. **Product:** A visual product or a performance that clearly reflects the best or most important cultural traditions of the country.
Center #4:	**History/Government Materials:** Center will be a table with a bifold or trifold poster that models a timeline. Posterboard Pens Markers Magazines **Task:** Create a timeline or other visual that shows the development of the country through the efforts of its leaders and the country's political struggles. **Product:** A poster or other representation that clearly reflects an accurate account of the country's history.
Center #5:	**Arts/Recreation Materials:** Center will be a table and an area for practicing. It could have a display case of sample cultural artifacts and a bifold or trifold of pictures of recreational activities. Posterboard Markers Magazines Paint Pens Small boxes Beads Glitter Ropes/sashes String Pins Clay **Task:** Create a product that reflects the best of the country's contribution to the arts and recreation of our world. **Product:** An arts product or a demonstration of a recreational activity.

Flexible Grouping

Students can be grouped throughout the year in various ways for various types of assignments. They can be grouped to represent *heterogeneous* readiness levels, learning styles, or interests, or they can be grouped by *homogeneous* readiness levels, learning styles, or interests depending on the goals and objectives of the lesson. Flexible grouping helps teachers avoid "tracking" students at certain levels or learning styles. Students can get to know more of their peers if they are required or inspired to become involved in group work with everyone in the class at some point during the year.

Differentiation Framework for Flexible Groups

This "Equalizer" from Carol Ann Tomlinson's (1995) *How to Differentiate Instruction in the Mixed-Ability Classroom*, is best utilized in this manner: (1) pretest students' understanding of a concept or skill, (2) teach or review the concept or skill, (3) assess student learning, and then (4) give assignments based on students' level of mastery. Students who need more time on the concept should be taught through activities on the far left, students who have mastered the information partially, should be taught through assignments in the middle column and students who have completely mastered the concepts should be taught through assignments from the far right. Below is my interpretation of "The Equalizer" (Northey, 2004).

1. Information, Ideas, Materials, Applications		
Foundational Activities are structured to help students master basic information about a concept or topic.	⟶ Activities are structured to require students to learn a concept or topic that is somewhat beyond basic information. Students can apply concepts.	**Transformational** Activities are structured to use the basic concepts or information about a topic in order to analyze, evaluate, or synthesize it in terms of other concepts and information.

2. Representations, Ideas, Applications, Materials		
Concrete Activities are structured so that students learn through the senses.	⟶ Activities are designed so that students use their senses to help them approach more abstract concepts.	**Abstract** Activities are created so that students can understand concepts without use of the senses.

3. Resources, Research, Issues, Problems, Skills, Goals		
Simple Activities are structured to include single concepts or ideas presented in as few words and steps as possible. Real world examples should be included to help make the information easier to understand.	⟶ Activities should include multiple concepts, but they must be highly organized with real world examples and modeling.	**Complex** Activities should include complex concepts and information requiring learners to independently discriminate between necessary and unnecessary information, determine fact versus opinion, make inferences and draw conclusions, and use induction and deduction.

4. Directions, Problems, Application, Solutions, Approaches, Disciplinary Connections		
Single Facet Activities should teach one concept until mastered.	⟶ Activities should be sequenced carefully to teach concepts in highly organized steps.	**Multiple Facets** Activities should include information imbedded in real world issues that have many interdisciplinary connections and parts.

5. Application, Insight, Transfer		
Small Leap Activities should require students to take one idea at a time.	⟶ Activities can require students to make greater leaps in connections between ideas, but with structure and modeling.	**Great Leap** Activities can require students to draw conclusions, make decisions, and engage in divergent thinking.

6. Solutions, Decisions, Approaches		
More Structured Activities should be highly structured and convergent.	⟶ Activities can be more open, but with parameters and a mix of convergent and divergent thinking.	**More Open** Activities can allow students to make decisions about product and process and answers can be divergent.
7. Planning, Designing, Monitoring		
Less Independence Activities may require more teacher assistance.	⟶ Activities can be more complex if the teacher can provide some help.	**Greater Independence** Activities should be structured so that students may work with very little teacher help.
8. Pace of Study, Pace of thought		
Slow Allow more time for fewer concepts.	⟶ Allow an average amount of time to master an average amount of information.	**Quick** Count on students to master information with one explanation and a few practices or applications.

(Northey, 2004)

Generic Strategies for Teaching *Math, Reading,* and *Writing Skills* Using "The Equalizer" to Flexibly Group Secondary Students

Take the following steps: (1) Pretest math, reading or writing skill (2) Teach a math, reading or writing skill or concept, (3) Assess student mastery of that skill or concept, and (4) Assign students activities using the specific content you are teaching. What follows are some generic activities I designed using Tomlinson's Equalizer.

1. Information, Ideas, Materials, Applications		
Foundational	—————————————▶	**Transformational**
Math: Reteach the basic math skill using a method that helps students connect the math skill with prior knowledge or that helps them make the abstract concrete. Give students several assignment sheets that allow them to practice using the skill as many times as necessary to help them reach mastery. Retest after each assignment sheet and 24 hours later. Add on skills and retest constantly.	*Math:* Give students simple word problems that require them to continue to practice applying the math skill they have just learned. Add other skills to word problems as appropriate. Use Exercises, Extra Practice or other sections that allow students to practice working the math problems represented by the skill.	*Math:* Give students multi-level real world or fuzzy math problems that require them to discriminate between useful and useless information, determine appropriate mathematical operations, and evaluate the appropriateness of procedures and answers. Use "For Extension or Enrichment" activities provided by most textbooks.
Reading: Reteach the reading comprehension skills by using examples that help students apply the comprehension skills to their frame of reference. Give students assignment sheets and short selections to practice the reading comprehension skills they have not mastered. Retest after practice and 24 hours until they have mastered the concept. Add on skills, practice, and retest constantly.	Reading: Ask students to independently read and answer questions in the textbook or questions generated by students or the teacher.	*Reading:* Students should begin a challenging novel study that includes having them keep a double entry journal critically reading for tone, mood, effect of author's style, symbolism, and the psychological intent of the work.
Writing: Reteach the writing skill in a limited writing assignment, e.g., one paragraph at a time. Reassess the writing skill within 24 hours. Continue to add on skills.	*Writing:* Ask students to independently plan and write compositions that demonstrate their understanding of basic writing strategies you have taught. Introduce strategies gradually.	*Writing:* Students write complex compositions responding to complex prompts in various writing modes.

2. Representations, Ideas, Applications, Materials		
Concrete	————————————▶	**Abstract**
Math: Use manipulatives, "hands-on," or kinesthetic method to teach or reteach simple mathematical concepts.	*Math:* Use manipulatives, hands-on, or kinesthetic method as necessary to help students transition to more abstract concepts within word problems. Use textbook practice problems.	*Math:* Require students to use abstract reasoning to solve complex word problems based on abstract uses of math. Use textbook enrichment problems and activities.
Reading: Give students simple selections that have clear and easily recognizable examples of reading comprehension skills, such as comparing and contrasting, determining author's purpose, identifying words in context, and comparing and contrasting. Give student several selections to practice comprehension skills. Provide graphic organizers for more abstract skills, such as inference and author's purpose, style, and tone.	*Reading:* Help students move toward abstraction by giving them graphic organizers to help them use comprehension skills to move toward critical analysis of information.	*Reading:* Ask students to infer and draw conclusions as they critically read selections above grade level. Require them to identify abstract concepts such as tone, mood, symbolism, and author's purpose and style.
Writing: Students use graphic organizers to help them organize their writing. Topics should be well-known to students frame of reference.	*Writing:* Students write to prompts that are based on topics within their frame of reference.	*Writing:* Students should write to prompts that require them to develop a tone, mood, sense of audience, purpose, and style.

3. Resources, Research, Issues, Problems, Skills, Goals		
Simple	⟶	**Complex**
Math: Make sure students can use basic math skills (addition, subtraction, multiplication, division). Show them how to make a word problem simple by underlining key words, phrases, and numbers. Spend time allowing students to practice breaking down a problem to make is easier to solve.	*Math:* Use a graphic method to help students identify critical elements in increasingly complex word problems. Use textbook practice problems, and challenge students to attempt to try enrichment problems and other challenging word problems.	*Math:* Ask students to solve highly complex real world word problems. Ask students to make up their own real world math problems based on their interests. Use textbook enrichment problems as available.
Reading: Assign students reading selections that are on their grade level and have simple plots so that they can build fluency and confidence in their ability to read independently.	*Reading:* Show students how to use graphic organizers, such a story map, a conflict analysis sheet, a organizer that helps students determine tone, etc. to analyze increasingly complex selections.	*Reading:* Require students to read selections with complex story lines, themes and styles.
Writing: Have students use simple organizational patterns and syntax to express themselves. Teach them to use correct grammar, usage, mechanics, and spelling (GUMS). They may need to spend some time practicing correct GUMS. Add more complex patterns as students master the simple ones.	*Writing:* Use graphic organizers to help students plan compositions that address more complex topics. Teach them complex organizational patterns and help them move from formula to more complex organizational patterns by using peer editing and teacher feedback.	*Writing:* Require students to vary syntax and use sophisticated diction as they fully develop their ideas. They should include sufficient details that flow smoothly through use of transitions.

4. Directions, Problems, Application, Solutions, Approaches, Disciplinary Connections		
Single Facet	⟶	**Multiple Facets**
Math: Teach one math skill at a time. Use a spiraling curriculum in which skills are constantly reintroduced and retested.	Math: Teach math skills that occur naturally together so that students can see the relationships more clearly.	Math: Ask students to note the relationships between math skills in order to form or solve multi-faceted real world word problems.
Reading: Teach discrete reading comprehension skills. Use short and easy reading selections, such as picture books to teach students a single reading skill. Use spiraling to add skills, reteach old skills and retest skills.	*Reading:* Ask students to independently use several reading comprehension skills as they analyze a selection on grade level.	*Reading:* Give students challenging selections that require them to apply reading comprehension strategies and critical reading strategies that help them evaluate that selection based on determined criteria.
Writing: Choose one writing technique or skill and give students feedback on their execution of that technique or skill in a short writing assignment.	*Writing:* Ask students to use multiple writing techniques and skills and use peer editing and teacher feedback to evaluate their use of those techniques or skills in a composition.	*Writing:* Require students to use a wide variety of sophisticated writing techniques and skills to develop a composition that is above grade level. They should be able to use appropriate terms to describe writing techniques and GUMS.

5. Application, Insight, Transfer		
Small Leap	————————————▶	**Great Leap**
Math: Emphasize mastery of single skills and concepts and take small steps when adding new ones. Make sure through assessment that students are transferring skills to application of those skills in word problems.	*Math:* Give students as much practice as necessary in applying discrete math skills to real world math problems. Use textbook practice problems until mastery.	*Math:* Plan activities that require students to apply discrete math skills to solve open-ended and fuzzy real world math problems. Use textbook enrichment and extension problems.
Reading: Emphasize mastery of single skills and concepts and take small steps when adding new ones. Make sure through assessment that students are transferring skills to the application of those skills to reading for understanding.	*Reading:* Ask students to read selection from their textbook or in grade level novels. Plan activities that require students to apply the discrete reading comprehension skills. Assess for understanding at a deep level.	*Reading:* Use classics or other rigorous reading practice that stretch students toward high levels of insight into author's use of style to develop a psychological intent.
Writing: Monitor small pieces of writing for application of discrete writing skills and GUMS.	*Writing:* Use prompts that ask students to use prior knowledge in order to practice applying discrete writing skills. Use peer editing and teacher feedback.	*Writing:* Use prompts that require students to show sophisticated insight and skill in developing compositions that demonstrate understanding of audience, style and organization for various purposes.

6. Solutions, Decisions, Approaches

More Structured	———————————➤	More Open
Math: Present information that is highly structured and convergent. Do not require students to determine process or product. Use assignment sheets and teacher input.	*Math:* Use structured activities, including assignment sheets that students can do on their own. Include examples, modeling, and opportunities to practice that help students move toward more open kinds of word problems.	*Math:* Use problem–based learning activities that require students to determine the following: what is the problem, what math skills are required to solve it, and what are appropriate answers?
Reading: Use assignment sheets and short selections to structure student learning. Use structured seminar (i.e., teacher controlled) to help students learn to write questions that move toward higher order thinking.	*Reading:* Use textbook selections and ask students to write answers to questions in textbook or write their own questions for seminar learning. Allow students to take some responsibility for leading seminars.	Reading: Use problem–based learning to require students to use high-level thinking skills such as synthesis and evaluation to respond to literature.
Writing: Use structured organizers and formula to help students learn basic skills. Use structured skill development exercises that transfer to real writing.	*Writing:* Help students use graphic organizers and formula to move toward more open methods of planning and composing.	*Writing:* Use creative writing, such as scenario writing to practice organizing and using details to reflect a style, purpose and awareness of audience.

7. Planning, Designing, Monitoring

Less Independence	———————————➤	Greater Independence
Math, Reading, and Writing: Make sure the teacher is available to give direct instruction and feedback. Do not make students wait too long to get help.	*Math, Reading, and Writing*: Students should be able to work on their own with less help from the teacher if the assignment is designed well. Expect students to need teacher input if assignments require students to move to more complex, abstract, or open-ended concepts and skills.	*Math, Reading, and Writing:* Students can work on their own, but the teacher should be available to consult with them to prompt them toward higher levels of thinking and reacting.

8. Pace of study, Pace of thought		
Slow	⟶	**Quick**
Math, Reading, and Writing: Plan on students taking more time to learn limited concepts and skills (i.e., aptitude is the amount of time it takes to learn something).	*Math, Reading, and Writing:* Students should take an average amount of time to master concepts and skills. These are the students for whom pacing guides are planned.	*Math, Reading, and Writing:* These students will be bored and frustrated if pacing is not geared to their ability to quickly grasp concepts and skills. After concepts or skills are presented, be prepared to offer engaging, and challenging opportunities to practice using new skills and concepts. Minimize reviewing.

Strategies for Teaching *Social Studies* and *Science* Using "The Equalizer" to Flexibly Group Students:

1. Information, Ideas, Materials, Applications		
Foundational	⟶	Transformational
Social Studies: Read a graph that shows social studies information. Explain three important facts the graph tells you.	*Social Studies:* Write a well-organized paragraph that explains the information on a social studies graph.	*Social Studies:* Read a social studies map and write a well-organized paragraph that explains the usefulness of the graph for analyzing topics such as: economics, land forms, politics, history, and culture.
Science: Make a data collection table to show information about the temperature in the classroom for 2 weeks. Use that table to find the average temperature for each week.	*Science*: Analyze a data collection table you have made on the temperature in the classroom. Write a paragraph explaining the conclusions you have drawn about what the data means and how you might use a data collection table for other experiments.	*Science:* Make a data collection table that enables you to test a hypothesis you have made about temperature.

2. Representations, Ideas, Applications, Materials		
Concrete	⟶	Abstract
Social Studies: Make a poster showing the five themes of geography.	*Social Studies:* Choose a country and write a report explaining how the five themes of geography are meaningful in terms of that country's history.	*Social Studies:* Write an essay explaining why the five themes of geography are critical to social studies.
Science: Make a barometer. Observe and record how it reacts to changes in air pressure in the classroom.	*Science:* Make a barometer, record pressure changes, and explain what kind of weather would be associated with each pressure you record.	Science: Make a barometer. Observe and record how it reacts to changes in air pressure. Evaluate how a barometer might be used to predict weather.

3. Resources, Research, Issues, Problems, Skills, Goals		
Simple	————————————————▶	**Complex**
Social Studies: Define and give examples of the following terms: history, geography, economics, government, and culture.	*Social Studies:* Explain in a well-organized composition why it is important to learn about the history, government, economy, geography, and culture of a country.	*Social Studies:* In a brief composition, explain the theme of relationships to your understanding of these concepts: history, geography, economics, government, and culture.
Science: Make a chart of the five major functions of the skeletal system.	*Science:* In a well-organized compostion, explain why knowledge of how the skeletal system works is important in our daily lives.	*Science:* Write a brief composition or make a graphic organizer explaining how knowledge of the functions of the skeletal system is relevant to performing at least three sports.

4. Directions, Problems, Application, Solutions, Approaches, Disciplinary Connections		
Single Facet	————————————————▶	**Multi-Facet**
Social Studies: Make a time line for a specific purpose.	*Social Studies:* Make a time line and rank order at last 3 critical events affecting the government of a country.	*Social Studies:* Make a time line and write an essay that explains the trends that were critical in the development of the economy, government, and culture of a country.
Science: With help from the teacher, a partner, or peers in a small group make a word web for the word "virus."	*Science:* Explain in a well-organized compostion how viruses reproduce and cause diseases and how scientists have dealt with them through history.	*Science:* Develop a method of identifying and explaining five viruses. Include what causes the virus, how it is spread, how the virus is tested, and if there are any other special features of the virus.

5. Application, Insight, Transfer

Small Leap	————————————➤	Great Leap
Social Studies: Read the chapter on Ancient Greece and define the key words in bold print. Use the new words in a sentence about Greece.	*Social Studies:* Read the chapter on Ancient Greece and rewrite the sentences that contain new words (i.e., the ones in bold print) in your own words (in other words, paraphrase those sentences).	*Social Studies:* Find a source of information written on a higher grade level for information about ancient Greece. Compare and contrast the information in the chapter in the textbook with the new information.
Science: Use information from the textbook to make a chart showing how you classify fungi based on how they reproduce.	*Science:* Make a Venn diagram to compare and contrast the types of fungi.	*Science:* Find an article that explains the work of environmentalists. Explain in an essay why an environmentalist would need to know a lot about fungi.

6. Solutions, Decisions, Approaches

More Structured	————————————➤	More Open
Social Studies: Develop a detailed study guide for the chapter on "The Culture of West Africa." Assign partners to read to each other and fill in the answers on the study guide.	*Social Studies:* Ask students to answer questions at the end of the chapter on "The Culture of West Africa."	*Social Studies:* Work alone, with a partner or in a small group to develop a creative method for demonstrating your understanding of the main ideas in the chapter on "The Culture of West Africa."
Science: Read the chapter about smog in the textbook. Make a poster that explains the different sources of pollutants.	*Science*: Write a report or use an art form (i.e., dance, drama, visual arts, music) to show the impact of pollutants on people and animals.	*Science:* Choose a creative method to explain the impact pollutants could have on the earth in the future.

7. Planning, Designing, Monitoring		
Less Independence	⟶	**Greater Independence**
Social Studies: Work with a partner or in a cooperative group to take double entry notes on the chapter titled, "Native American Traditions." Identify and define the key concepts explained in the chapter.	*Social Studies:* Work with a partner or by yourself to identify the main ideas and sub-ideas in the chapter on "Native American Traditions." Write the information in outline form.	*Social Studies:* With a partner or small group, find sources that extend the information in the chapter on "Native American Traditions." Add information to the textbook chapter.
Science: Use a levels guide to read the chapter on "The Senses."	Science: Read the chapter on "The Senses." Take Cornell notes to show your understanding of the main ideas.	*Science:* Read the chapter on "The Senses" and choose one of them on which to become an expert. Find at least two sources to teach you more about that sense. Make a report to the class about your findings.

8. Pace of study, Pace of thought		
Slow	⟶	**Quick**
This is the same for Math, Reading, and Writing	This is the same for Math, Reading, and Writing.	This is the same for Math, Reading, and Writing.

Adjusting Questions in Whole Class Discussion

Teachers should ask questions that challenge all levels of students in order to meet their cognitive needs. A good tool for this purpose is the "Question Matrix" (or "Q Matrix") designed by Chuck Weiderhold. This matrix, featured in Patricia E. Blosser's (1973) in *Handbook of Effective Questioning Techniques,* is a great template for helping teachers ask questions that address all levels of Bloom's Taxonomy. This is a useful template to keep handy until you get in the habit of using these levels automatically.

How to use this grid:

♦ Suggestion 1: As you prepare to have an interactive discussion with your students, you may want to use this matrix to help you compose questions from as many of the boxes as reasonable for your topic and the amount of time you have available. Writing the questions ahead of time will help you balance your questioning to address lower to higher levels of thinking.

♦ Suggestion 2: If you would rather not have preset questions because you want to keep the conversation about a topic more spontaneous and in-tune with the directions the students would like to go, you could use this matrix to guide your question stems *while* you are having an interactive discussion with students. If you want to monitor your ability to pose questions in a balanced manner, you might check a box, each time you use that question stem.

♦ Suggestion 3: As you are making a test to determine students' mastery of a topic, you might use this matrix to differentiate levels of difficulty for that test.

Q Matrix (Question Stems)

1. What is?	2. Where When is?	3. Which is?	4. Who is?	5. Why is?	6. How is?
7. What did?	8. Where When did?	9. Which did?	10. Who did?	11. Why did?	12. How did?
13. What can?	14. Where When can?	15. Which can?	16. Who can?	17. Why can?	18. How can?
19. What would?	20. Where When would?	21. Which would?	22. Who would?	23. Why would?	24. How would?
25. What will?	26. Where When will?	27. Which will?	28. Who will?	29. Why will?	30. How will?
31. What might?	32. Where When might?	33. Which might?	34. Who might?	35. Why might?	36. How might?

Task Cards

Cards can be used to tell students exactly what they are to do to master the goals and objectives of a unit of study. Giving students various cards or a series of cards is an excellent way to differentiate instruction for a whole class. Sandra Kaplan has an excellent model for gifted students for ensuring that tasks are sufficiently deep and complex and that thinking skills are higher order (Kaplan, Gould, & Siegel, 1995). Her *Flip Book* is a useful way to structure assignments easily for process, content, and product differentiation. From *The Flip Book* by Sandra Kaplan:

Elements of Differentiated Learning Experiences

Thinking Skills	*Differentiation of Content*	*Research Skills*	*Products*
Basic Skills: ♦ Compare and contrast ♦ Categories ♦ Sequence ♦ Identify attributes *Other Basic Skills:* ♦ Determine cause and effect ♦ Recognize relationships ♦ Summarize *Critical Thinking Skills:* ♦ Differentiate fact from fiction ♦ Differentiate relevant from irrelevant ♦ Judge with criteria ♦ Prioritize ♦ Gather evidence for support *Other Critical Thinking Skills* ♦ Note ambiguity ♦ State/test assumptions ♦ Judge authenticity *Creative Thinking Skills* ♦ Redesign ♦ Combine ♦ Substitute ♦ Add to	*Depth:* ♦ State trends ♦ Note patterns ♦ Identify/note details ♦ State ethical considerations ♦ Define unanswered questions ♦ Identify the rules ♦ State the generalization, principle or big idea *Complexity:* ♦ View from different perspectives ♦ Recognize multiple points of view ♦ Define over time	*Gathering Information and Using Resources:* ♦ Use pictures ♦ Experiment ♦ Use a computer ♦ Use video and audio technology ♦ Read/use a book ♦ Use the new media Interview *Organizing Information:* ♦ Draw conclusions ♦ Paraphrase ♦ Outline	♦ Dramatize ♦ Make a model ♦ Survey and graph ♦ Write ♦ Illustrate ♦ Construct something ♦ Make a chart ♦ Develop a photo or picture essay ♦ Teach a lesson ♦ Debate

(Kaplan, 1995)

Part of Lesson Using Task Cards

Unit Theme: Conflict

Topic: Asia: China and Japan

Generalizations:
- Conflict is reflected in the relationships of landforms to create various climates.
- Conflict occurs as the traditional is displaced by the modern.
- Conflict occurs between economic philosophies (communism vs. capitalism).
- Conflict is revealed in traditional and modern arts and recreation.
- Conflict occurs internally (within a country) and externally (between countries).

Lesson 1

Level 1	Level 2	Level 3
Thinking Skills: Knowledge and comprehension	**Thinking Skills:** Knowledge, comprehension, gather evidence, recognize relationships, determine cause and effect.	**Thinking Skills:** Gather evidence to support, recognize relationships, determine cause and effect.
Process: Work individually or with a partner.	**Process:** Work individually or with a partner.	**Process:** Work individually.
Product: Make a glossary of key vocabulary words and key places. Illustrate key places.	Product: Take Cornell notes on the chapter on landforms. Write questions from the notes and make a quiz for another student or students.	Product: Write a composition explaining at least three ways the mountains of East Asia affect the rivers and the lowlands.
Research skill: Use the cart of books on China and Japan, a computer, the textbook, magazines and newspaper articles	Research Skills: Use the cart of books on China and Japan, a computer, the textbook, magazines, and newspaper articles	Research skills: Use the cart of books on China and Japan, a computer, the textbook, magazines and newspaper articles
		Differentiation for Gifted: In the paper, note patterns, identify principles, and note details.

Small Group Differentiation

Small group differentiation is about dividing the class into groups for specific purposes and differentiating the roles and actions of students in those small groups.

Literature Circles

Literature circles can be used for fiction and nonfiction in literature-based classes or in other content area classes. To use literature circles implement the following steps:

Planning:

♦ Step 1: Choose a short selection that all students can read to teach them the process of Literature Circles (Teach the process at step 3).

♦ Step 2: Select the roles you would like students to use for Literature Circles, usually four or five roles are sufficient.

Here are some of the roles from which to choose with brief descriptions (in order of most often used):

- Discussion Leader—Begins and ends the discussion and keeps it going. He/she may have the responsibility of asking the questions he/she has written to stimulate discussion or to determine the agenda for the discussion. He/she may be responsible for determining the next reading assignment and the rotation of the roles.

- Illustrator—Draws a picture that represents an important aspect of the text being studied. Everyone wants this job because it seems easy, but even though artistic talent is not necessary, the work is graded, and it should reflect higher order thinking skills, organization, and neatness.

- Vocabulary Highlighter—Chooses important words that must be understood in order to understand the text. He/she must write the page number, why he/she chose the word, and what the word means.

- Passage Illuminator—Chooses a passage to discuss with the group, and decides how that passage should be shared, such as one person reading it aloud, each person reading it silently, or all reading it together aloud or silently. The passage could be selected because it contains critical information, confusing information, especially well-written information, or for other reasons.

He/she should write the page number on which the passage appears in the text.

- Summarizer—This student summarizes the text noting important events or concepts.

- Connection Maker—Connects the text with himself/herself and real life events or other texts.

- Globe Trotter—Provides information about the places in which the text is set. Uses maps, globes, etc. to help students visualize the location of the events or other aspects of the text.

- Investigator—Uses research to broaden the understanding of the events or concepts developed in the text.

Implementing:

- ◆ Step 3: Go over each role you choose to use and assign them one of two ways.

  - Actually put students in groups of four or five and number off. Ask the one's to take one role, the two's another and so on.

  - Or, have everyone practice each role one at a time.

- ◆ Step 4: Everyone reads the same selection and practices the roles. Students share with the whole class what they have done in their various roles. The class discusses how well the students performed the various roles.

- ◆ Step 5: Determine a method for students to choose or be assigned a text to study.

  Note: If you are doing various novels, you can do "book stations" that each have a copy of a book. Show students a method of learning about the book. You may want to make a selection sheet that has the following suggestions or questions:

  - read the back cover or jacket cover

  - look at the picture on the front

  - read the first page,

  - do the five-finger test for unknown vocabulary

  - think about why the book is interesting

  - rank order the book choices.

The teacher could then group students according to their first choices if at all possible.

♦ Step 6: Assign students to groups based on their choices or your needs for them, and then let them know how many times the Literature Circle will meet, so that they may divide the text into segments. Ask students to determine roles, or count-off to determine roles (i.e., one's become Illustrators, two's become Discussion Leaders and so forth). The teacher should continuously circulate around the room to monitor the activities.

♦ Step 7: Important advice: for accountability purposes, each role should be evaluated on a per meeting basis, and an overall project inspired by the text should be assigned in addition to the daily role assignments. Also strongly recommended is revolving roles, permitting each student a chance to do each role once or twice.

You can download forms and get a great deal of information from the following Internet sources: www.literaturecircles.com and http://fac-staff. seattleu.edu/kschlnoe/LitCircles.

Study Groups

Study groups are somewhat different from interest groups, although an interest group can be set up like a study group; however, a study group is often set up apart from the whole class and can exist as separate from the class. There are several types of study groups as follows:

- Issues based
- Readers and writers group
- Book discussion
- Topic-centered

Study groups can be organized as follows:

♦ Step 1: Invite a small group of students (no more than 6) to come together for one of the purposes stated above.

♦ Step 2: Establish the schedule and the place the group will meet, such as in the classroom, in a designated area, or in another location.

♦ Step 3: Help students establish the "ground rules" for the group such as:

- Begin and end at a certain time during the period.
- Establish meaningful roles for each group member.
- Communicate respectfully among group members.

- Assure that all members are accountable for their work in the group.

- Keep information confidential if it is sensitive.

- Participate actively (no slacking).

- Decide if leadership will rotate or will be one person for the duration of the group.

- Step 4: Determine what kind of product you want the group to present at the end of the amount of time you establish for them to meet.

- Step 4: Monitor the work of the group on a regular basis and make certain all members are on track for turning in the product that results from their work together.

Example:

Students who were highly interested in writing formed a writers' study group that met after school once per week. The leadership rotated and the product was a piece of writing to be submitted for publication. The English teacher provided supervision and guidance, but the students ran the group. Each person agreed to bring in a piece of writing for each weekly meeting. Students helped each other improve each writer's work by making respectful suggestions.

Cubed Discussion Groups

This method of small group differentiation adds an engaging dimension to differentiation because it makes chance a part of the process. Discussion groups can use cubes in the following ways:

- Each group has a different cube (i.e., the group is formed based on the type of cube it will use).

- All groups have the same questions on their cubes.

- Each group has several cubes from which to choose.

Cubes can be made by enlarging the enclosed pattern on heavy paper and typing questions onto the pattern, or they can be made by finding a box and gluing questions to it. Make sure the box is completely square, however, or students will not be able to roll adequately.

Pattern for Cubed Discussion Groups

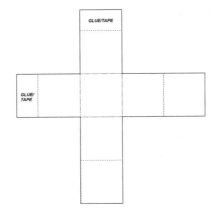

Example:

The following example blends the concepts of Grant Wiggins and Hugh McTighe (1998) in *Understanding by Design* and Harold Gardner's "Entry Points" related to the Multiple Intelligences (1993).

Cubed Discussion Groups: Based on the Six Facets of Learning and Gardner's Entry Points (Learning Styles)

The teacher should group students into five learning styles groups based on where she thinks students fit in terms of Gardner's "Entry Points" (defined below). Students could use this strategy when the teacher wants students to work somewhat independently in groups during a unit in which the teacher wants students to read a longer fiction or nonfiction work. Students should divide the work into six parts (at least), so that this unit will last for at least six classes. Students should read each part for homework and should come to class prepared to use the cubes to guide their production of evidence of understanding of the what they have read. During class, the teacher should give each group two cubes or one cube that has two sections on each side.

The five "Entry Points" are as follows:

- ♦ Narrative (learning through story)—Students with these cubes may either discuss answers orally or write their responses to the prompts on the cubes. If students discuss orally, they should at least write a sufficient reflection about the discussion.

- ♦ *Logical/Quantitative* (learning through numbers/logic)—Students with these cubes should include a written product, such as graphic organizers or charts.

- ♦ *Foundational* (learning through theory/meaning)—Students with these cubes should turn in a written product.

♦ *Aesthetic* (learning through the arts)—Students with these cubes should turn in or perform aesthetic products in class. If a product is performed, it should include a brief commentary.

♦ *Experiential* (learning through hands on)—Students will role play and perform skits to answer their prompts; therefore, they should write at least one reflective paragraph about the experience of role playing.

Instruct students to use the cubes to decide how they will discuss their selection for each session. Students respond to the assignment as it appears on the side of the cube that comes up when they roll it.

The teacher should make five sturdy cubes, one for each "Entry Point." Each cube will address the "Entry Point" and each side of the cube will address one of the "Six Facets of Understanding" (explanation, interpretation, application, perspective, empathy, self-knowledge). Each facet will be divided in terms of the "Realm of Knowledge" (K) and in terms of the "Realm of People and Emotions (PE)." You can draw a line to show the two realms (one cube) or you could make a separate cube for each realm under each "Entry Point" (two cubes per group).

For a full discussion of the Six Facets of Understanding, read *Understanding by Design* by Wiggins and McTighe (1998).

How to use these cubes:

After you give each group one or two cubes, tell them to decide who rolls first, second, third, and fourth. Decide if you want them to address "Realm of Knowledge" and then "Realm of People and Emotions," or if you want them all to answer "Realm of Knowledge" prompts first, and then go to "Realm of People and Emotions" next.

Here is how it looks:

♦ Step 1: Teacher or students decide the order in which they will roll the die.

♦ Step 2: The person rolls the die and responds to what comes face up on it. (Tell them: "No rerolling if they don't like what it says.") In some cases the person rolling the die will have sole responsibility for responding, and in other cases the person rolling the die will lead the group in an activity. In some cases the person will find out what to do and begin doing it quietly while the next person rolls and gets his/her assignment.

Suggestions:

• Practice rolling your dice before you give them to the students. Make sure the same prompt doesn't come up every time.

- Tell students to cover several of the prompts on the die, and do what makes sense if the same prompt comes up too many times.

- Each group and each prompt is different; however, the general guidelines help with accountability.

- Each group member is responsible for handing in concrete evidence that they have worked on the cube.

- Remember that differentiating for learning styles can get noisy; therefore you need to decide if you can accommodate all five "Entry Points." If your classroom does not allow for moving and many people talking, you may want to use only certain "Entry Points" on your cubes.

Narrative Entry Point

Knowledge (**K**) People and Emotions (**PE**)

- Explanation

  K Use your knowledge of the selection to convince your peers to read it.

  PE Explain what motivates the main character or narrator to make decisions that have an impact on the plot of the story.

- Interpretation

  K Explain how the setting of the work affects the characters or the situations.

  PE Explain how internal and external conflict affect the characters' actions in the work.

- Application

  K Use your knowledge of the work to summarize the main points so far.

  PE Explain how you connect with the main character's thoughts and feelings.

- Perspective

  K Evaluate the effect of the author's attitude on the work so far.

  PE Evaluate the author's use of situations and language in the work to determine his/her attitude toward the characters.

- Empathy

  K Explain your feelings about a character and his/her actions.

  PE Explain what advice you might give to a student who is similar to a character in the work.

♦ Self-Knowledge

K   Explain how your perspective may limit or enhance your understanding of the work.

PE   Express how your biases or prejudices affect your feelings about the characters or a situation in the work.

Logical-Quantitative Entry Point

♦ Explanation

K   Use your knowledge of the work to form a theory about what makes it worth reading.

PE   Use your understanding of the characters to form a theory about what makes the work so appealing to students your age.

♦ Interpretation

K   Make a map of the elements of the selection revealed so far.

PE   Complete a graphic organizer on "Conflict" to show your understanding or the conflict in the work so far.

♦ Perspective

K   Design a graphic method to show how the author's attitudes are revealed in the work.

PE   Design a graphic method to show the differing perspectives of the main characters in the work.

♦ Empathy

K   Design a series of symbols that reflect various feeling states. Write the names of the characters so far and put symbols by their names to indicate their predominate feeling state so far.

PE   Make a chart comparing characters in the book with people you know or know about. Include a method for showing how they are alike emotionally.

♦ Self-Knowledge

K   Choose five categories of characters traits (e.g., friendly, honest) and make a diagram comparing yourself according to those traits with at least two of the characters.

PE   Brainstorm to develop a list of prejudices or biases people can have. Rate each character in the work and rate yourself on where you fit in at range from 1 to 10.

Foundational Entry Point

♦ Explanation

K Explain the basic issues (include setting and characters) in the work so far.

PE Explain the methods the writer uses to reveal the characters so far (include direct and indirect methods of characterization).

♦ Interpretation

K Find at least five connotative words, images, or details that reveal the author's attitude or tone in the work so far. Note any shifts in attitude or tone.

PE Find at least five connotative words, images, or details associated with specific characters that reveal the author's attitude toward those characters.

♦ Application

K Choose five words from the story so far to make an advertisement or headline about the work. Explain why those five words were essential (do not consider articles like "the" and "a" as one of the five words.)

PE Summarize the work so far for a friend or younger person. Write at least one paragraph explaining how your word choice and details reflect an accurate statement of the work so far.

♦ Perspective

K Evaluate how the author's use of diction, imagery, details, language, and syntax reveal his tone. List at least one example from the five categories and explain how these add up to create the tone.

PE Evaluate how the author's tone affects the overall effect of the work so far.

♦ Empathy

K Make a list of at least ten highly emotional words, details, or images the author uses in the story to reveal important information. Explain why each word is on the list.

PE Make a list of at least ten highly emotional words used to describe or used in reference to at least one of the characters. Explain why each word is important to reveal the character.

♦ Self-Knowledge

K Write a summary of the story so far and analyze how your word choice and details reveal your perspective about the work so far.

PE Make a list of at least five words that show how your perspective is similar or different from the main character's perspective. Explain why you chose each of the words.

Aesthetic Entry Point

- Explanation

  K Use your knowledge of the elements of fiction or nonfiction to create an artistic representation of one of those elements as it is found in the work.

  PE Use your knowledge of the way your peers interact to help you create an artistic representation of the way the characters interact with each other in the work.

- Interpretation

  K Use an artistic method (dance, music, visual art) to show how the setting of the work affects the characters or the plot of the story.

  PE Use an artistic method to show how the conflict (internal or external) affects the characters' actions in the work.

- Application

  K Use your knowledge of the work to create an artistic presentation about the action so far.

  PE Show artistically how you relate to the main character's thoughts and feelings.

- Perspective

  K Use an artistic method to show how your knowledge of the issues in the novel affects your point of view on that issue.

  PE Use an artistic method to compare and contrast your attitude toward the work with the author's attitude toward the work.

- Empathy

  K Create an artistic product that reveals your knowledge of the feelings of the main characters.

  PE Create an artistic product that reveals how real people in your life feel similarly to or differently from the main characters in the work.

Experiential Entry Point

- Explanation

  K Use your knowledge of the story to present a three-minute commercial selling it to a movie-maker. Perform for the class or write a reflection.

  PE Use role-playing to explain the main issues in the work. Perform for the class or write a reflection.

  Interpretation

K Perform an improvisational skit (with people or puppets) that reveals your understanding of how the setting affects the characters or the situation. Write a reflection.

PE Stage an argument between two characters that may or may not have occurred in the work. Write a brief reflection about what you learned.

♦ Application

K Choose a scene from the work and act it out (or do reader's theater) and write a reflection about how acting out the action helped you understand it better.

PE Join the action of one of the scenes in the work. Role-play a conversation with one of the characters. Write a brief reflection of what you learned.

♦ Perspective

K Role play a scene from the work from several different characters' perspectives. Write a reflection about whose perspective is most like yours.

PE Choose a variety of perspectives from the following list: an old person, a mother, a father, a policeman, a teacher, or others you choose. Role-play a scene from the work. Write about how at least two of these types of people would feel about the scene.

♦ Empathy

K Role play talking to one of the main characters. Tell him/her how you feel about him/her so far, and if you can/cannot identify with their issues.

PE Pretend you are a social worker, counselor, or psychologist. Role-play a session with one of the main characters. Write a reflection of what you learned.

(Northey, 2004)

Cooperative Groups

Spencer Kagen is one of the best sources for Cooperative Group ideas. One of the most useful strategies is the "Jigsaw" method (1992), which can be used to get information to students in a wide variety of ways such as a written text, a film, an experiential activity, a picture or graph, and others. These are the steps to take:

♦ Step 1: Decide what you want to teach and determine what primary sources will help students best learn the concepts or information.

You may use a variety of sources so that students may choose what they want to explore based on interests, readiness, or learning styles.

♦ Step 2: Divide the class into groups of four to six. This group becomes the "home group." You may divide them or have them choose their own groups depending on how you have chosen the learning materials and activities.

♦ Step 3: Determine how many and what kinds of sources of information you want the groups to explore. The number of sources should match the number of members of the group.

♦ Step 4: Have group members either number off or choose a source of information in which they are interested or that matches their learning style. For instance, one source of information could be experiential so that a kinesthetic learner may want to learn the concepts or information through that method.

♦ Step 5: Give each learning source a number that matches the number of a group member and ask like numbers to join each other to learn about the concept from their chosen or randomly selected source. This new group is the "Expert Group." For instance, all the one's may get together to do an experiment, all the two's read the same article, the three's view a film together, and the four's look at a picture or graph together.

♦ Step 6: After the "Expert Group" has experienced their activity or read their article, they should discuss with each other the best method to help members of their "Home Group" learn the concepts or information.

♦ Step 7: Experts rejoin their "Home Group," and then take turns teaching each other what they learned from their own source.

♦ Step 8: Home groups discuss their overall learning and reflect on the new concepts or information.

Ordered Sharing

This idea comes from Geoffrey and Renate Caine who promote brain/mind constructivism and have a wealth of tools for teachers to boost higher level thinking skills and to improve school climate. Their web address is: http://cainelearning.com for much more information.

"Ordered Sharing" is one of their many ideas. Teachers can use it with groups of six to eight students. I suggest if the teacher cannot lead each group, she/he should have a responsible student start and end the discussion while she/he floats to monitor comments.

- ◆ Step 1: The teacher chooses a topic related to his/her unit of study.
- ◆ Step 2: Students get into groups of six to eight. Any grouping strategy would work.
- ◆ Step 3: The teacher explains the topic, and then asks students to think about it.
- ◆ Step 4: The teacher (or group leaders) says "whoever is ready to begin should do so," and when everyone has had a chance to comment, the group may speak about the topic freely.
- ◆ Step 5: After everyone has spoken, the teacher or group leader asks, "What did you notice? How did it go? What did you learn? Etc.

Individualizing Instruction

Research Projects

One of the easiest ways to individualize learning is to ask a student to choose a topic of interest in order to write a paper or produce a product on it to show learning. There are various research methods and documentation methods, but they are all about having students

- ◆ determine a topic or thesis,
- ◆ seek and find information about the topic,
- ◆ take notes on that topic for a purpose and an audience,
- ◆ use those notes to develop an organized product, and
- ◆ use a method to credit sources. And a possible
- ◆ find a way to share the information with the class.

Here is a generic example:

Research Paper Syllabus

1. Choose a topic you would like to explore.
2. Find a minimum of three sources, including one person you can interview about your topic.
3. Begin taking notes from your sources and thinking about the main ideas for your paper.
4. Develop a *thesis statement* that your research on the topic can prove.
5. Organize your ideas into an outline.

6. Write a three to five page paper using parenthetical documentation to cite your sources in the body of the paper.

7. Include the following parts for the following points:

attractive cover sheet	5 points
outline	10 points
parenthetical documentation	10 points
body	50 points
works cited page	15 points
note cards	10 points

How to take notes:

1. Get a package of small index cards.

2. Make a bibliography card for each source. (Your teacher or media specialist will shoose a specific documentation style.)

3. Make note cards as follows:

   A. At the top of each card make a parenthetical documentation notation (i.e., author's last name or shortened title if no author and page number—no commas).

   B. Write down *exactly* what is written in the sources or said by the person you are interviewing. *Note:* You will paraphrase or synthesize information into your paper, but not on the card. You must be careful not to plagiarize (i.e., using the writer's exact words without quotes and parenthetical documentation or using the writer's thoughts without parenthetical documentation).

   The only ideas you do not document with parenthetical documentation are commonly held ideas (i.e., ideas you find in three or four places) or conclusions you draw from the research.

   C. Write *one* idea per card. Do not think you need to fill up the card. One to three sentences should be enough per card. You will need several cards per page of your paper.

General Outline Form:

I. Introduction

   A. Catchy opening

   B. Thesis statement (Major Claim)

   C. Summary of main ideas (Claims)

II. Main Idea #1 (Claim 1)

   A. Support #1

    B. Support #2

    C. Support #3 (Minimum)

    D. Wrap up (Warrant—draws a conclusion about the claim and support for it)

II. Main Idea #2 (Claim 2)

    A. Support #1

    B. Support #2

    C. Support #3 (Minimum)

    D. Wrap up (Warrant)

IV. Main Idea #3 (Claim 3—Minimum)

    A. Support #1

    B. Support #2

    C. Support #3 (Minimum)

    D. Wrap up (Warrant)

V. Conclusion

    A. Restate the thesis

    B. Restate the summary of main ideas (Claims)

    C. Draw a conclusion about your topic, but do not add any new claims or support. (Major Warrant)

How to Organize your note cards in preparation for writing:

1. Alphabetize your bibliography cards.

2. Look at your outline and read each note card to determine under which Roman numeral the card will most likely fit. Put the Roman numeral at the top left hand side of the card.

3. After you have decided where each card fits under each Roman numeral, decide where the card fits under the capital letters: A, B, or C, etc. Put the appropriate letter next to the Roman numeral at the top of the left hand corner of the card.

4. Stack your cards in the order they will occur in the paper. The bibliography cards go last. You can copy them in alphabetical order on a piece of paper to form your Works Cited page. Use rubber bands or large paper clips to separate the cards by their Roman numerals.

How to Write your paper:

1. Whenever you use information from a note card, you must paraphrase or synthesize that information (put it in your own words or draw conclusions about it) and use parenthetical documentation to label each idea or group of ideas you use from your sources. Also, if you use the same source for an entire paragraph, you should only make the parenthetical notation at the end of that paragraph, not after every sentence.

2. Do not forget to use transitions to make your report coherent and do not leave any parts out.

3. Read over your paper carefully to edit for GUMS errors.

How to Make the Works Cited Page:

1. Write Works Cited at the top of the page.

2. Use *correct indentation* and a correct form to note your sources.

Remember that writing thorough, interesting, and accurate information that proves your thesis is most important; however, the next most important skill is how well you organize and follow a consistent format for citing sources.

The Tic-Tac-Toe Menu

This activity is adapted from Susan Winebrenner's (1992) *Teaching Gifted Kids in the Regular Classroom* (this page (p. 64) can be photocopied).

Teachers create a menu of activities, such as the Tic-Tac-Toe Menu below, and ask students to choose a determined number of activities from that menu. Teachers can choose any similar kinds of verbs as the actions for students to take and can leave some boxes blank so that students can supply their own ideas.

Example:

Tic-Tac-Toe Menu

1. **Collect** ideas and facts about a topic of interest to you.	2. **Teach** the class something about a topic in which you are interested.	3. **Compare/Contrast** your topic of study with another topic and note ways they are different and alike
4. **Film/Photograph** something of interest from your topic and present it to the class.	5. **Graph/Data Base** information from your topic to share with the class.	6. **Demonstrate** something about a topic to show what you learned.
7. **Survey** other students and interested people to determine how they feel about your topic.	8. **Dramatize** something you have learned about your topic.	9. **Predict** how your topic will change our world or make a big difference in the next 10 years.

Directions: Choose three activities from the tic-tac-toe design. Make sure you get tic-tack toe.

Activities: #____, #____, #____, #____(optional)

Student's Signature _____ Date_____

Curriculum Compacting

Compacting can be used for individual students or for groups of students. It requires the teacher to do three things: (1) Assess what a student or students already know about a unit of study. (2) Make a plan that addresses any gaps a student or students might have in the concepts, skills and knowledge covered in the unit of study, and (3) Determine enrichment activities that will deepen students' concept development, knowledge and skills related to the unit of study.

Example Lesson: Fast Track Math:
Assignment to Students:

Each math unit is divided into discrete math concepts. For instance, Chapter 4 in our textbook is about "Statistics" with 4.1 being "Circle Graphs," 4.2 being "Bar Graphs," and so on. You will read the directions for each "discrete math skill," and then you will work five problems in the "Exercises" section of the textbook. After you have worked those problems, you will bring them to the teacher who will check them. If you get all of them right, or only miss one, you will move on to the next discrete lesson. If you are unable to work the problems on your own, you should see the teacher for verbal instruction. At the end of each unit, you will take a "Unit Test" to determine if you are ready to solve enrichment problems. If you do not master the material (80% correct), you should do five more problems in the areas you did not master and then retest. If you master the material, you will work on enrichment problems from the textbook or provided by the teacher. When you have adequately completed these problems, you will start on the next unit. Continue to work at your own pace.

Independent Study

Independent study is a great way to engage students in self-directed exploration of one of their interests. This method is especially useful for students who consistently stay ahead of the rest of the class. An independent study is set up as collaboration between the teacher and the students. The teacher invites students to determine interests they would like to study. Next, the teacher helps students determine the method they will use to investigate their interests, and what product they will develop to show learning, and how that product will be evaluated. It is a good idea to set time lines, and have check-points to monitor students' progress.

Use this contract for students who have selected a topic on which to do an "Independent Study."

Independent Study Contract

Name:_____ Date of Contract:_____

Topic of Study:_____

Method of Study:_____

_____

List of possible sources:

    1.

    2.

    3.

    4.

    5.

(You must use at least 2 primary sources)

Proposed Product (You may choose from among the following: research report, video documentary, visual arts product, musical product, dance product, drama product, or other with approval.)

Due Date:_____ (The product will lose 10 points for each day it is late.)

The product will be graded as follows: 25 points for each of the following:

   ♦ Accurate information

   ♦ Sufficient information

   ♦ Technical accuracy (i.e., sources correctly credited, neatly formated, and aesthetically pleasing)

   ♦ Creativity

I will do my best work: _____ Date:_____

                                 Student's Signature

Learning Contracts

Learning contracts are agreements between students and teachers that determine what work will be done for what grade. The contract explicitly outlines the activities of the unit and the standards by which the product determined as evidence of learning will be evaluated. Students can contract for an A, B, or C. Teachers usually do not allow students to contract for less than an average grade, although some students may fall short of meeting the requirements of the contract and get less than they contracted to receive. (Some teachers may not want to contract for anything below an A.) The contract should be highly specific in terms of activities, when the work is expected, the quantity of the work, and the quality of the work.

**Example Contract: Academic Enrichment for Students
Who Do Not Master Content with Regular Pacing**

Student Contract

I _____ agree to do the following to receive an "A" in
my Academic Enrichment class:

- ◆ Work independently and quietly on the concept or skill I am assigned.
- ◆ Master information or skill with a minimum of 95% correct on assessments.
- ◆ Work individually, with a partner, or in a small group to learn concepts or skills I have trouble understanding.
- ◆ Make the best use of my time by staying on task.
- ◆ Move to the next concept or skill when I have mastered the concept or skill on which I am working.
- ◆ Be truthful about what I know about a concept or skill.
- ◆ Ask for help when I do not understand.

If I follow this contract, I will receive the following:

- ◆ An "A" for my participation in the class.
- ◆ A ticket back to my elective when I have mastered all concepts or skills.

Student: _____ Date: _____

Teacher: _____ Date: _____

Parent: _____ Date: _____

Generic Academic Enrichment Work Schedule for Students Who Do Not Master Concepts or Skills with Regular Pacing

Name: _____ Period: _____

Date Started: _____ Date Ended: _____

Objective to master: _____

And/or specific concept or skill to master:_____

Textbook Chapter Number and Title: _____

Pretest Information (scores, etc.) _____

Session #1: Reteaching by (check one or add on):

___ Coaching—circle one: (student partner, teacher, tutor)
Name of coach:_____

___ Write or orally explain the steps or define the concept and give examples

___ Student-developed questions and answers

___ Practice assignments

___Other—explain:_____

Assessment 1 Scores/Grades: _____

If Not Mastered:

Session #2: Reteaching by (check or add):

___ Explore the concept or skill through experiential method. Explain the method:_____

_____

___Use a game or simulation Describe: _____

_____

___Other—explain:_____

_____

Assessment #2: Information—scores/grades: _____

If student does not master…

Session #3: Reteaching by (Describe, e.g., after school tutoring, computer instruction, etc.): _____

_____

_____

Assessment #3: _____

_____

_____

After three reteaching sessions and three assessments, if student still has not mastered the concept or skill explain why:

Apprentice/Mentorship

Students work with various adults, such as parents, a school media specialist or other school personnel or with a community agency to pursue a special interest in which the adult or agency has expertise. The teacher and student work with the mentor to determine the process by which the student will learn and the product that will be evidence of that learning.

Many districts have elaborate apprenticeship programs. If you would like to set one up, you should make sure you develop a **process** that clearly outlines your program. Do the following:

1. Explain what an apprenticeship is, and who is eligible to participate.
2. Provide a step-by-step outline of how students should apply, how employers or mentors should monitor students' work, how much time must be spent in the apprenticeship (i.e., some states have guidelines for amount of time necessary), what work products are required, when that work is due, and how the work will be evaluated.
3. Explain the benefits of the program for all involved.
4. Provide contact information.

You should also develop a **contract** that would include the following:

♦ Student's Name

♦ School

♦ Job Title

♦ Job Site

♦ Student's Responsibilities

♦ Employer or Mentor's Responsibilities

♦ Teacher in charge or Program Coordinator's responsibilities.

♦ Parent or Guardian's responsibilities

♦ Dates of the contract

♦ What students are expected to learn from the apprenticeship

Everyone involved including the Principal of the school should sign and date the contract.

Personalized System of Instruction and Computer-Aided Personalized System of Instruction

Personalized System of Instruction (PSI) is a method of learning in which students pace themselves through course materials. At the beginning of a course, the teacher gives students study questions and problems that guide the students' work. Peer tutors who are in more advanced courses help students work their way through the requirements in order to master the material (Keller, 1968)

Computer-Aided Personalized System of Instruction (CAPSI) adds the dimension of the virtual capabilities of computers (Kulik, Kulik, Bangert-Downs, 1990). CAPSI is similar to PSI in that students are self-paced and the instructor gives study questions and problems; however, with this method of instruction students within the same course evaluate each other's work to determine if a student has mastered an assignment. The teacher spot checks to make sure peers are fair and accurate in their assessment of one another. See Joseph Pear's article, "Teaching and Researching Higher Order Thinking in a Virtual Environment" online at http://home.cc.umanitoba.ca/~capsi/capsipapers2.htm.

Miscellaneous Strategies for Whole Class, Small Group, or Individual Differentiation

Special Strategies That Boost Thinking and Creativity Derived from the Business World

Strategies that boost creative problem solving abound in the business world. Many educators have borrowed and continue to borrow great ideas that connect schools with that world. Here are some wonderful strategies that can enhance the thinking and creativity in a differentiated classroom.

Brainstorming

Alex F. Osborne (1953) invented the concept of brainstorming in the 1930s to help businesses use their creative powers and imagination to create products, solve problems, and make profit. He invented it as a way to get those who were less likely to make suggestions to feel free to speak up. Brainstorming has four basic rules:

- No criticism is allowed. Evaluation of an idea comes later.
- "Free-wheeling" is promoted. Wild and off-the-wall ideas are fine; it's easier to calm them down than to generate them.
- The more ideas the better.
- Combining ideas and adding to others' ideas is helpful and welcomed.

Here are the 4 stages of brainstorming:

- State the problem or issue
- Restate the problem or issue

- Brainstorm solutions that address one or more of the restatements of the problem.

- Evaluate solutions

Here are some steps to take in the classroom to use brainstorming to solve a problem (adapted form the business model by Osborn):

1. **Orientation**: Tell students about the problem and let them know that the class will be using a technique called *brainstorming* to solve it. Explain the four rules of brainstorming so that everyone feels comfortable sharing. Feel assured that the class is prepared to be respectful of others' ideas as they work together to solve a problem. (The problem can be from any topic of study, and if it is a real world problem that crosses content areas, the better.)

2. **Preparation**: Make sure your classroom is quiet and energized for thinking and responding to a teacher planned or student generated problem.

3. **Analysis**: Break down the problem so that everyone sees the relevant issues that should be addressed.

4. **Hypothesis**: This is where the brainstorming happens.

5. **Incubation**: Stopping to let the ideas sink in and allow time for insight and thoughtfulness.

6. **Synthesis**: Putting ideas together to determine possible solutions.

7. **Verification**: Evaluate the solutions and choose the best.

From: www.ciadvertising.org

SIT (Systematic Inventive Thinking or ASIT–Advanced Systematic Inventive Thinking)

This concept of fostering creativity is an adaptation of ARIZ or TRIZ (Russian acronym for Theory of the Solutions of Invented Problems), a method discovered by Genrich Altshuler (1988). He believed that one may learn from examining existing creative ideas in order to analyze the logical problems that they have in common. By determining the problem *patterns* one can determine a group of "thinking tools" that help you develop new creative ideas. TRIZ is highly complex and seems to have been replaced by the more user friendly SIT. ASIT (Advanced SIT) has five universal techniques: unification, multiplication, division, breaking symmetry, and object removal. Go to www.Start2Think.com or to "Systematic Inventive Thinking Innovation" at www.sitsite.com for more information about how to become trained in this exciting method of learning to solve problems systematically and creatively.

SCAMPER (Osborn, Eberle, and Michalko)

Michael Michalko (1991), inspired by the concept of checklisting from Alex Osborn's book *Applied Imagination: Principles and Procedures of Creative Problem Solving*, presented the ideas that became SCAMPER in his seminal work on creative thinking, *Tinkertoys* (1991). Bob Eberle (1996) adapted Michalko's ideas into the process he named SCAMPER, which takes students through the following checklist toward creative problem solving:

Take an object:

- ♦ **S**—Substitute some aspect.
- ♦ **C**—Combine the elements of the object with something.
- ♦ **A**—Adapt or alter something about the object.
- ♦ **M**—Modify (magnify, minify) or change something about it.
- ♦ **P**—Put some part of it to other uses.
- ♦ **E**—Eliminate or reduce something about it.
- ♦ **R**—Reverse or rearrange something about it.

To use SCAMPER take these two steps:

- ♦ Step 1: Determine a challenge or subject.
- ♦ Step 2: Ask SCAMPER questions about each step of the challenge and see what happens.

For example:

Take a stapler

- ♦ **S**—Substitute colored, flavored, edible candy for the staples.
- ♦ **C**—Combine it with a slab of thin gummy paper-thin candy.
- ♦ **A**—Adapt it so that it is disposable (so that it doesn't get too icky).
- ♦ **M**—Modify it so that it so that the candy staples will not spoil easily (melt or dry out).
- ♦ **P**—Put it to another use as a candy shooter.
- ♦ **E**—Eliminate the need for the staples to bend in order to stay in the gummy sheets.
- ♦ **R**—Rearrange the insides so that the candy staples will come out easily and won't break.

Wouldn't students love this product!

Scamper can even be used in English/Language Arts to discuss a story. Go online at www.discover.tased.edu.au/english/scamper.htm or www.brainstorming.co.uk/tutorials/scampertutorial.html for more ideas. There are SCAMPER contests and lots of examples on how to use this creative and fun process, some call SCAMPERING.

Lateral Thinking

Conceptualized by Edward de Bono, Lateral Thinking is a systematic method of improving creative thinking based on techniques that are brain-based. De Bono (1985) conceptualized "6 Thinking Hats" as a method to help problem solvers do one thing at a time and to be able to label exactly what they are doing. Each hat represents an aspect of problem solving.

The hats are as follows:

- White: This hat is objective. This hat is only concerned with the facts.
- Red: Emotions rule
- Black: The "devils advocate," conservative, careful
- Yellow: Positive, cheery
- Green: Growing and creating; wanting new ideas
- Blue: Organization

How to Use this Concept

Teachers could use the hats one at a time sequentially to talk about a problem or concept. Or they could use the hats all at the same time with different students wearing different hats and reacting to a problem from the perspective of the hat they are wearing at the time. The hats could be rotated so that everyone experiences responding from each hat. Because there are six hats, each group could have six students or you could do a fishbowl with six students in the middle discussing the issue while the rest of the class observed and evaluated the discussion.

Ideas from Business That Boost Creativity

If you want a great list of ideas to boost your creativity and that of your students, search an online article by Chris Jones, "Creativity Boosters" available from www.cma-i.org/members/m2m/m1m_02nov.htm.

Concepts That Are Organic to Differentiation

FLOW

Mihaly Csikszentmihalyi is one of the most creative thinkers of our time. He conceptualized the idea of "Flow," which explains the state of well-being that comes from pursuing creative and productive work. Go to www.austega.com/education/articles/flow.htm. According to Csikszentmilhalyi this is what it means to be in a state of flow:

1. Completely involved, focused, concentrating—with this either due to innate curiosity or as the result of training

2. Sense of ecstasy—of being outside everyday reality

3. Great inner clarity—knowing what needs to be done and how well it is going

4. Knowing the activity is doable—that the skills are adequate, and neither anxious or bored

5. Sense of serenity—no worries about self, feeling of growing beyond the boundaries of ego—afterwards feeling of transcending ego in ways not thought possible

6. Timeliness—thoroughly focused on present, don't notice time passing

7. Intrinsic motivation—whatever produces "flow" becomes its own reward

The effectively differentiated classroom should bring all children into the state of *flow*.

Workshop

The concept of a classroom that becomes a workshop where students are engaged individually, in partnerships, or in small groups in meeting specific goals and satisfying specific needs within a content area, is well-described in Nancie Atwell's work. As students in her classroom learn to read and write, the teacher becomes like a supervisor who provides a method of monitoring and accountability within that content area. The monitoring procedures of note are as follows:

- ♦ daily process grid

- ♦ letters to other students or to the teacher in journals

- ♦ individual conferences with the teacher

- ♦ presenting work as it is accomplished to the natural audience in the classroom

Students can learn any content area from this Reading and Writing Workshop.

Special Time-Saving Strategies for the Differentiated Classroom: RICE and Education Sponge Activities

RICE

With so many activities going on in the differentiated classroom, students may get confused about what to do next or fail to understand their assignment. This strategy encourages students to stay actively involved in learning even when this happens.

R—Remember what the teacher said (model how to remember–close your eyes and visualize her hear in your mind)

I—Imagine logically what the directions would be for the task.

C—Check with a classmate.

E—Ask the "Expert" of the day (at the beginning of the period, appoint a student who is responsible for paying close attention to directions).

Educational Sponge Activities

Educational Sponge Activities are those that "absorb" time for students who finish work at different rates. See the following web address for an extensive list of activities: http://tepserver.ucsd.edu/courses/tep129/EducatoinalSponges.pd, or go to Google and type: Educational Sponge Activities, which offers you the option of viewing in html or pdf formats.

Two Frameworks
for Differentiating Instruction

There are two other frameworks for differentiating instruction worth mentioning here. Although I have not used the technique myself, teachers may be interested in exploring these ideas as they think about differentiation. One is "Complex Instruction" developed by Elizabeth Cohen (1986) at Stanford University and the other is the "Parallel Curriculum" conceptualized by Carol Ann Tomlinson, Sandra Kaplan, Joseph Renzulli, Jeanne Purcell, Jann Lappien, and Deborah E. Burns (2001).

Complex Instruction is a cooperative learning strategy that is structured to ensure learners work interdependently at their most challenging level. The model requires teachers to flexibly group students of varying intellectual ability for the purpose of solving real world complex tasks. Students become increasingly more responsible for their own learning as they rely on the various strengths of fellow group members to get a problem solved or the work done. To learn more about this strategy see Cohen's book *Designing Groupwork Strategies for the Heterogeneous Classroom* (second edition).

The other framework to consider is the Parallel Curriculum, which can help teachers plan lessons that not only address the core curriculum defined by their districts, but can also help them consider three other equally important curricula. The three other curricula are as follows: the curriculum of connections (linking concepts within the school setting and/or with other elements of the real world), the curriculum of practice (encouraging students' to develop expertise and to apply course objectives to real world employment), and the curriculum of identity (helping students see how a concept within the content of a course relates to them personally). For more information see *The Parallel Curriculum* by Carol Ann Tomlinson et al. (2001).

Summary

Teachers can differentiate for whole classes, within groups, and for individuals. It is a matter of choosing which strategy works the best for your students and for your content. Consider your space limitations and tolerance for noise as whole class differentiation, especially for learning styles, can be very busy and noisy. If you are attempting to accommodate kinesthetic learners, you have to have room for them to move. If you want to accommodate for auditory learners, there has to be sound. If you do not want all that going on in the room at one time, you could teach the same objective to whole classes through the various learning modes and intelligences during different class periods or during different segments of a block.

If you want to be able to teach to all learning styles, you may want to consult with teachers who have strengths in areas with which you have the most difficulty thinking of ways to present. For example, if you have no musical ability, but several of your students learn best through music, you might want to ask the chorus teacher for some suggestions on how to present concepts using music. Better yet, you could team teach a concept with him/her or integrate your academic objectives with his/her artistic ones.

As far as differentiating for readiness is concerned, I have always heard that teachers should teach to the top of the class; however, word choice, pacing, and expectations must fairly challenge, but not over-challenge each student. Teachers should match instruction and assessment as closely as possible to students' readiness and abilities. Differentiating products after you have delivered the same instruction to the whole class may be the only way to differentiate for readiness in some cases. Teachers should be prepared to reteach concepts and skills to students who simply did not "get it" through the whole class instruction or the practice. They may be able to add scaffolding during a guided practice or individual practice segment of the class.

To maximize the motivation of secondary students to learn grade level content, teachers need to clearly understand the developmental issues with which they are dealing. For instance, middle school teachers, knowing that their students love to work together and that boy-girl groups can be tricky, are able to plan excellent group activities. High school teachers should know what is "cool" to do with high school students and what they would think is too silly. Knowing these developmental issues will help teachers plan best strategies for their students. Also, knowing the interest of an individual unmotivated learner can turn him/her around if he/she is permitted and encouraged to work on that interest in an individual contract or apprenticeship.

Remember that the first rule is that the process you chose should fit the children first and the content second.

4

Assessment: Differentiating Product

This chapter contains information and suggestions about how to differentiate the product so that assessment will be fair to all students..

Assessment includes:

- ◆ Determining a product that is acceptable evidence of mastery of concepts and/or skills.

- ◆ Evaluating that product to determine if the student has mastered concepts and or skills.

Assessment procedures vary widely. The most common assessment procedure to determine ability is the "Standardized Test," usually a multiple choice test, but sometimes an essay test. Standardized tests are helpful when districts want to have some idea of how their students are achieving in comparison with students from other districts or among schools in the same districts. Also colleges use them to objectively determine the capabilities of the students they are accepting into their programs.

However, teachers who are committed to differentiation know they need to determine assessment procedures that most closely match their teaching and the needs of their students; therefore, they use a wide variety of techniques that allow for a wide variety of student abilities, interests, and styles to demonstrate mastery of skills and understanding of concepts. They also need to develop measurement tools that are not only quantitative (i.e., number or percentage of correct answers), but those that are also holistic, analytical, and qualitative.

Assessment can include any of the following major categories:

- ◆ Question-based assessment
- ◆ Problem-based assessment
- ◆ Performance-based assessment
- ◆ Affective domain-based assessment
- ◆ Self and/or peer-based assessment

Question-Based Assessment

Questioning is one of the most useful methods of differentiating assessment. Oral and written responses to varied levels and types of questions help teachers formally and informally get an idea of how the class and individual students are understanding the concepts of the unit of study. Questions can be used for various purposes, such as:

♦ Teachers can pose essential questions at the beginning of units to guide students' learning,

♦ Teachers can pose interactive discussion questions when they and their students are determining their prior knowledge of a subject or exploring a subject in depth during an interactive lecture.

♦ Teachers can use questions and prompts to make written quizzes, content tests, and unit tests. Multiple-choice questions can determine right answers and essay or short answer prompts can assess divergent thinking.

♦ Teachers and/or students can ask each other discussion questions in seminar settings where students are required to answer questions by referencing the text to support their claims and responses.

Questioning Strategies

Essential Questions

♦ Have more than one answer

♦ Are engaging and challenging

♦ Often cross over from one area of learning to another

♦ Occur naturally in real world contexts

Examples of Essential Questions:

♦ Language Arts: How does an author's use of various stylistic techniques have an impact on their audience?

♦ Science: How does the scientific method help solve medical problems?

♦ Social Studies: How does the movement of people affect their culture?

♦ Math: How does the order of operations affect answers to math problems?

Interactive Questions

- ◆ Can be used for voluntary response
- ◆ Can be used for demand response
- ◆ Can be used for formal evaluation or informal evaluation (If used for formal evaluation, some written record must be maintained.)
- ◆ Should allow wait time (5–7 seconds)
- ◆ Should not be leading
- ◆ Should not be judged favorably or unfavorably
- ◆ Should be expressed positively if possible
- ◆ Can be based on various taxonomies and theories, such a Bloom's taxonomy, Richard Paul's *Critical Thinking*, and others.

Examples of categories of questions and stems:

- • Comparing and contrasting—example: How is one thing different or the same as another thing?
- • Observing—example: What do you see when this happens?
- • Ordering—example: What patterns do you notice when this happens?
- • Communicating—example: Can you summarize your findings?
- • Categorizing—example: How would you group these things?
- • Applying: Example: How did your evidence help you determine the answer to your question?
- • Inferring—example: How do you know this is correct?
- • Relating—example: What factors caused this to happen?

Here is another list that is especially good for mathematics questioning:

- ◆ *Problem Comprehension*: Can students understand, define, formulate, or explain the problem? Example: What is this problem about?
- ◆ *Approaches and Strategies*: Do students have an organizational approach to the problem or task? Example: Where could you find the needed information?
- ◆ *Relationships*: Do students see relationships and recognize the central ideas? Example: What is the pattern?
- ◆ *Flexibility*: Can students vary their approach if one is not working? Example: What else have you tried?

♦ *Communication*: Can students describe or depict strategies they are using? Example: Can you explain this process to someone who does not understand it?

♦ *Curiosity and Hypothesis*: Is there evidence of conjecturing, thinking ahead, and thinking back? Example: Can you make a prediction about what will happen next?

♦ *Equality and Equity*: Do all students participate to the same degree? Example: Have you discussed all the answers with your group?

♦ *Solutions*: Do students reach results: Example: Is that the best answer?

♦ *Examining Results*: Can students generalize from their answers? Example: Is there a real world situation where this information would be useful?

♦ *Mathematical Learning*: Did students learn some mathematics from this activity? Example: What mathematical concepts did you use to solve this problem?

♦ *Self-Assessment*: Do students evaluate their own processing, actions, and progress? Example: What were your strengths and weaknesses?

From Assessment Alternative in Mathematics, a booklet from the California Mathematics Council and EQUAL

Use question stems from **Bloom's Taxonomy**:

♦ Knowledge: Who, what, where, when, and how?

♦ Comprehension: Explain the meaning of this in your own words.

♦ Application: How is this an example of _____?

♦ Analysis: Outline or diagram the_____.

♦ Synthesis: How would you create/design a _____from what you have learned?

♦ Evaluation: Do you agree?

Use question stems that promote **Reading comprehension**:

♦ Inference and Conclusion: Which idea *best* explains…?

♦ Compare and Contrast: How is _____different from_____?

♦ Fact and Opinion: Which of these ideas is fact?

♦ Cause and Effect: What is the *most likely* cause of…?

♦ Sequencing: What happened first in the story?

♦ Author's Purpose: What purpose did the author have for using_____in this story?

♦ Vocabulary in Context: In this sentence…,what does the word_____mean?

♦ Main Idea: What is the main idea of this selection? What would be a good title for this selection?

♦ Literary Techniques: Identify the part of speech and how it helped the writer show…?

Here is a list of question categories and stems that can be used in **seminar questioning:**

♦ Questions of clarification: Example: What do you mean by_____?

♦ Questions that probe assumptions: Example: You seem to be assuming_____. Do I understand you correctly?

♦ Questions that probe reasons and evidence: Example: How do you know?

♦ Questions about viewpoints and perspectives: Example: Did anyone see this issue another way?

♦ Questions that probe implications and consequences: Example: What are you implying by that?

♦ Questions about the question: Example: How can we find out?

From Paul, Binker, Jensen, & Kreklau (1987), *Critical thinking handbook: 4th-6th Grades: A guide for remodeling lesson plans in language arts social studies and science.*

Two seminar methods worth discussing here

♦ Socratic Seminar

♦ Fishbowl

For both of these strategies, teach students Art Costa's *3 Levels of Questions* (Costa, Kallick. 2000) as follows:

♦ Level I Questions: Answers are found "right there" in the text. There is one right answer. Example: How many stepsisters did Cinderella have?

♦ Level II Questions: Answers are found "between the lines" of the text. Students must use inference and/or must draw conclusions to determine a range of best answers. Example: Why was Cinderella's stepmother so mean to her?

♦ Level III Questions: Require students to think of issues "beyond the text" that references to the text help answer. Example: What does the story of Cinderella teach us about step parenting?

Socratic Seminar

Socratic Seminar (also known as *Paidaiea* Seminar) is a wonderful method of discussion a fiction or nonfiction print or nonprint work. The rules for the Socratic Seminar are:

- ◆ Students sit in a circle or around a table facing each other. (For a very large class, I have kept students as they are seated—we adapt.)
- ◆ Students must respond respectfully to each other.
- ◆ Students do not need to raise their hands to be called on by the teacher; however, they should maintain close eye contact with the speaker so that they know when they might have a turn to comment.
- ◆ Students must use standard English when they respond to a question or comment.
- ◆ Students must reference the text when they are answering a question.
- ◆ Students and or the teacher may determine the questions, which should be open-ended (Level II and III questions are best).
- ◆ Student's responses can be best scored by rubric.
- ◆ Responses should be monitored, and students should understand that their responses will be evaluated.

Fishbowl (In Steps):

1. Students form an inner circle of chairs and an outer circle. The inner circle is called the *fishbowl*. Ask one group of students to sit in the outer circle and another group to sit in the fishbowl.

2. Each student should be prepared to ask questions based on a print or nonprint work of fiction or nonfiction. Students in the fishbowl are to answer questions that students in the outer circle ask them. (Limit the number of questions to two per student. Students who have not written questions should not be allowed to participate.)

3. Students outside the fishbowl should listen carefully to the discussion of the students in the fishbowl so that they know when to ask the next questions.

4. Students outside the fishbowl should not participate in the discussion occurring in the fishbowl.

5. Students in the fishbowl do not need to raise their hands, they just answer, but they should not interrupt anyone or talk while someone else is talking.

6. Students in the fishbowl should discuss the questions asked by students outside the fishbowl. More than one student should comment on the

question. Statements like "I agree with _____." do not count as responses.

7. The teacher or another scorekeeper will keep a record of who participates. It is a good idea to limit the number of times a student can answer. Students can lose points for dominating a discussion.

8. After one group has been in the fishbowl for about 30 minutes, the group who has been in the outer circle should trade places with them and continue the discussion for another 30 minutes.

Problem-Based Assessment

Rather than using questioning, some teachers organize units or even their entire curriculum around solving different types of problems. Students' abilities to solve problems related to the curriculum become the method of assessing mastery of concepts and skills embedded in those problems. There are several excellent methods of utilizing problem-based learning or assessment in the classroom. The methods discussed here are:

- The Problem-Solving Matrix
- Ford-Harris Matrix based on Banks and Bloom's Taxonomy
- Problem Based Learning
- The Six-Step Problem Solving Method
- Scenario Writing

The Problem-Solving Matrix Types

Teachers can assess students' work for any unit of study by asking them to choose assignments from a matrix. What follows are three examples of how teachers can design matrices for assessment purposes. The following have combined various theories to form a matrix of assignment choices (see examples of each): (1) June Maker (1996) demonstrates how a continuum of problem types can be combined with Gardner's Multiple Intelligences, (2) Ford-Harris (1999) Matrix combines Bloom's Taxonomy with James Banks (1997) levels of culturally sensitive curriculum design, and (3) Lorin Anderson et.al. (2000) combine an updated version of Bloom's taxonomy with "Knowledge Dimensions."

(1) The Problem Solving Matrix

Maker (1996) uses five problem types as defined below:

Parts of Problem	Type I	Type II	Type III	Type IV	Type V
Problem	Clearly defined	Clearly defined	Clearly defined	Clearly defined	Find the problem, fuzzy, ill defined
Solution	Right Answers	Best Answers	Answers vary	Answers vary	Answers vary
Method	Clearly determined	Range of methods	Range of methods	Discover a method	Discover a method

In the generic matrix that follows [adapted from Maker's matrix by Northey (2004)], teachers ask students to individually or in groups choose a box or boxes of the matrix as their assessment assignment. [Note: To best utilize this matrix, it is helpful to understand Art Costa's Levels of Questions (see in "Questioning Strategies," page 153).]

A Generic Problem-Solving Matrix
That Can Be Adapted for a Specific Unit of Study

Type I	*Type II*	*Type III*	*Type IV*	*Type V*
Multiple Intelligence: Linguistic				
◆ Make a list of terms, define, and give examples. Or ◆ Answer Level I questions in which correct answers can be found in the text.	◆ Answer Level II and III questions, which require inference and conclusion. Or ◆ Write a report on the topic (answer a prompt). Or ◆ Make the information into a story. Or ◆ Write Seminar questions at Level II or above.	Write a story, a report, a play, a poem, or use another linguistic method to solve a clearly defined problem related to the unit of study.	Discover the best linguistic method to show your understanding of the essential questions and big ideas related to this unit.	Discover a linguistic method for solving a fuzzy or ill-defined problem such as a real world issue related to this unit. The solution(s) should demonstrate mastery of concepts and skills determined in the unit of study.
Multiple Intelligence: Logical Mathematical				
Use a graph or chart to show relationships among categories in the text.	Use bullets, graphic organizers, databases, thinking maps, or other methods to show the logical relationships among unit concepts that must be understood through inference and conclusion.	Use a range of graphic methods to show understanding of the main issues from the unit.	Discover a logical or mathematical method to solve a clearly defined problem associated with the skills and knowledge from this unit.	Discover a logical or mathematical method to solve an ill-defined problem inspired by this unit of study. Solutions should show mastery of concepts and skills that are objectives of this unit.

Type I	Type II	Type III	Type IV	Type V
Multiple Intelligence: Spatial				
Draw a picture or make a three-dimensional product that represents key concepts or ideas from this unit.	Draw a picture or make a three-dimensional product that shows ability to draw conclusions and inferences about concepts in this unit of study.	Choose from a range of spatial products to show your understanding of essential questions and big ideas from this unit of study.	Discover a spatial method that helps you solve a clearly defined problem associated with this unit of study.	Discover a spatial method that helps you solve an ill-defined problem associated with this unit of study.
Multiple Intelligence: Musical				
Make up a song or use a song you already know to help you understand or remember key terms and concepts from the unit of study.	Make up a song or use a song you already know to demonstrate your understanding of key concepts from the unit of study.	Use a range of musical methods to demonstrate your understanding of essential questions and big ideas from the unit of study.	Discover a musical method to solve a well-defined problem associated with the unit of study.	Discover a musical method to solve a fuzzy problem associated with the unit of study.
Multiple Intelligence: Bodily Kinesthetic				
Make up a dance or movement to help you understand or remember key concepts from a unit of study.	Make up a dance or movement that shows you understand key concepts from the unit of study.	Use a range of bodily kinesthetic methods to show you understand essential questions and big ideas from the unit of study.	Discover a bodily kinesthetic method to solve a well-defined problem associated with the unit of study.	Discover a bodily kinesthetic method to solve a fuzzy problem associated with the unit of study.
Multiple Intelligence: Interpersonal				
Use your ability to work with others to help you understand or remember key concepts from the unit of study.	Use your ability to work with others to help you draw conclusions or infer answers to questions from the unit of study.	Use a range of methods of working with others to show your ability to draw conclusions and make inferences about key concepts in the unit of study.	Discover a method of working with others to solve a well-defined problem associated with this unit of study.	Discover a method of working with others to solve an ill-defined problem associated with this unit of study.

Type I	Type II	Type II	Type IV	Type V
Multiple Intelligence: Intrapersonal				
Use your ability to work independently to help you understand or remember key concepts from the unit of study.	Use your ability to work independently to demonstrate the ability to draw conclusions and make inferences about concepts from the unit of study.	Use a range of independent strategies to demonstrate your understanding of essential questions and big ideas from the unit of study.	Discover a method of working independently to solve a well-defined problem associated with this unit of study.	Discover a method of working independently to solve a fuzzy problem associated with this unit of study.
Multiple Intelligence: Naturalist				
Make a diorama that shows a connection between key terms and concepts and natural phenomena or things from nature. Or Use items from nature, such as beans or sticks to help you understand or remember concepts from the unit.	Use your knowledge of nature to help you draw conclusions or make inferences about key concepts in the unit of study.	Use a range of natural products or natural problem solving to help you understand essential questions and big ideas from this unit of study.	Discover a naturalist way of solving a well-defined problem associated with this unit of study.	Discover a naturalist way of solving a real-world problem associated with this unit of study.

Ford-Harris Matrix

The Ford-Harris Matrix utilizes Bloom's Taxonomy and James Banks' (1987) Four Levels of approaches to designing a curriculum that is sensitive to racial and cultural diversity. This method is especially useful for integrating Social Studies and Language Arts content areas. The levels are:

Level I: The Contributions Approach: Students gain only superficial knowledge of racially and culturally diverse groups. Students learn about holidays, heroes, and discrete cultural elements.

Level II: The Additive Approach: New perspectives, content, themes, and ideas are added to the traditional (typically less diversified) curriculum; however, the basic structure of that curriculum is unchanged, and students fail to understand how the majority culture interacts with racially and culturally diverse groups.

Level III: The Transformation Approach: The structure of the curriculum is changed to allow students to experience how concepts, content, themes, and perspectives are perceived from racially and culturally diverse groups. Educators deliberately include and attempt to understand and incorporate the views of racially and culturally diverse groups.

Level IV: The Social Action Approach: Students are presented with social issues associated with racial and culturally diverse groups. The curriculum empowers them to make meaningful contributions or to determine actions that could help solve problems associated with those groups.

(2) Ford-Harris Matrix Using Bloom-Banks Framework
(Concept: Social Injustices—Stereotypes and Prejudice)

Knowledge	Comprehension	Application	Analysis	Synthesis	Evaluation
Level I Contributions					
Name three songs that were popular among slaves.	Make an outline of events leading to the Civil War.	Create a model of the underground railroad.	Examine how stereotypes about minority groups contribute to slavery.	Write a story about the contribution of Hispanic Americans to the music industry.	Critique the work of a famous American Indian artist.
Level II Additive					
List three factors that contribute to prejudiced beliefs.	After reading a biography about a famous person of color, summarize the social barriers that the person faced.	Find a book or song that discusses the problems of racial prejudice in society.	Compare and contrast the writing of W. E. B. Dubois and Booker T. Washington on issues of racial discrimination.	Write a play about the Spanish Inquisition.	Write a paper explaining why you think it is important (or not important) to learn about prejudice.
Level III Transformations					
Describe how slaves might have felt being held in captivity	Explain why American Indians use folk tales and story-telling as a means of coping with oppression.	Read the essay "What America Means to Me." Write a paper showing how members of a minority group might respond to this essay.	Predict how our nation would have prospered without slave labor. What other forms of labor could have been used?	Develop a survey regarding students' experiences with prejudice in their school or their community.	Assume the identity of a plantation owner or a slave. From that perspective, write a story outlining the difference between your life and the ideal of liberty and justice for all.

Level IV Social Action					
Explain what you would have done during the 17th century to end slavery?	List some ways that the media contribute to our perceptions of minority groups. What can be done to improve how the media portray minorities?	Review three to five sources on affirmative action, then write and submit an editorial to a newspaper describing your views on this topic.	Spend a day (or week) observing and analyzing how minority groups are treated at the mall. Share the results with storeowners.	Form a school club whose goal is to create a sense of community and respect in the school building.	Examine school policies to see if democratic ideals are present. Write a new school policy and share the findings and recommendactions with ad-ministration.

From Ford-Harris (1999). *Multicultural Gifted Education*. Retrieved on December 15, 2003, from http://www.coe.ohio-state.edu/dyford/Lessonplans/ford-harris.matrix.htm

(3) The Taxonomy Table

(Adapted from *A Taxonomy of Learning, Teaching, and Assessing* 2001)

Teachers can use this matrix for any unit to write assignments that move students to higher order thinking.

Knowledge Dimension	Remember (Recognize and recall)	Understand (Interpret, classify, infer, compare, explain)	Apply (Implement, execute)	Analyze (Organize, differentiate, attribute)	Evaluate (Critique, assess)	Create (Plan, produce)
Factual Knowledge						
Conceptual Knowledge (generalizations, theories, big ideas)						
Procedural Knowledge (techniques, methods)						
Meta-Cognitive Knowledge (strategies, cognitive tasks, self-knowledge)						

Note: Bloom's taxonomy has been updated to show new hierarchy of educational objectives. The Dimensions of Knowledge are parallel (not hierarchical).

Problem-Based Learning

Problem-based learning is more than a strategy; it is a manifestation of a philosophy about how students learn. This philosophy assumes students learn best if they are given chances to create meaning given certain broad ideas, goals, or objectives. Problem-based learning asks students to solve real world problems, which are most often ill-formed or "fuzzy" as compared to typical academic problems, which are constructed to help students learn discrete and compartmentalized concepts and skills.

In order to design a problem-based unit, teachers should take the following steps:

- ◆ Step 1: Determine what goals or objectives you would like to achieve.

- ◆ Step 2: Find a real-world situation or create a situation that will require students to achieve your stated goals and skills. Examples of places to find interesting situations: newspaper, song lyrics, advertisements, radio, television, personal experience.

- ◆ Step 3: Ask yourself questions like these in response to the situation:

  - • Is there a problem in this situation that could be solved by someone?

  - • What exactly *is* the problem?

  - • What skills are needed to solve the problem?

  - • What information is needed to solve the problem?

  - • What concepts would students learn as they attempted to solve this problem?

  - • Is this situation appropriate for my students?

  - • Will this situation engage my students?

  - • Can the problem be solved or at least lead to possibilities?

- ◆ Step 4: Decide how to present the situation to your students. Create a role, situation, and problem description (or let students figure out what the problem is).

Here is a good template:

Role (be sure this is an authentic problem solver for the situation):

Your are…

Example: a meteorologist.

Situation (stated in concrete terms, appropriate for age group, authentic, and engaging):

You have been...

Example: noticing over the past few years that some of the plants you were used to seeing in the spring were either not blooming or blooming sooner than you expected. Also the heavy winter coat your Aunt Sarah bought you in 1995 has stayed in the closet every winter and you're wondering if you ought to give it away to a charity. You have read that some scientists say climate is changing because of certain chemicals in the atmosphere, and you wonder if our climate has changed already. If it has changed, what does that mean for your life and the life of our planet?

Problem Description

Give students the following ideas for question stems to help them state the critical issue to be resolved and the criteria for determining if the solution is appropriate.

How can I...so that...   Or

How can I...taking into account... Or

How can I...being sure to...

Example: How can I find out possible explanations for what I am noticing so that I can plan a way to address these changes in my environment?

- Step 5: Involve the students in the following steps:

  1. Teacher presents situation to students

  2. Teacher allows time for student investigation and inquiry (including: searching for information in the media center; finding authentic sources in the community; using the teacher as a resource of direct instruction, authentic assessment, and evaluation of ideas; group collaboration)

  3. Students present their solutions

  4. Teacher and students evaluate the solutions and debrief

If you prefer to use a different template, try this alternative:

- Step 1: Find a situation from the newspaper or other source. Make a copy of it or show it on an overhead projector so that all students can read it.

♦ Step 2: Ask students in whole class or small group discussion to determine: What is the central problem embedded in the situation?

♦ Step 3: When the class has reached consensus or decided to consider different aspects of the problem, ask them to decide how they as students (their role) could work together or individually to plan a way to solve the problem. In the best case, they might even work authentically to solve the problem or call attention to it so that those who have the authority can solve it.

Author note: Problem identification and solution provide a great reason for students to practice authentic argumentative writing skills.

Six-Step Problem Solving

This strategy is useful for real world problem solving in all content areas. It is a wonderful skill that students can use for the rest of their lives. Teachers and students can find interesting problems in newspapers, in journals, and even in the daily life of a school. It is a great strategy for content integration because most real problems cross content lines.

Step I: **Challenges**

♦ Teacher or students determine a current problem or a future problem on which they will work. Example: What can be done to improve the eating habits of young people?

♦ Students brainstorm challenges to solving the problem. Students should try to think of at least five challenges. Example: 1. Proliferation of fast food restaurants; 2. Seductiveness of advertisements in magazine and on television; 3. Many food choices easy to fix, but poor in nutritional quality; 4. Young people passively watch television or play video games instead of participating in active pastimes; 5. Obsession with thinness.

Step II: **Focus on the Underlying Challenge**

♦ The team discusses the identified challenge in order to determine which challenge, if solved, might solve the other challenges. Use the "four part structure" (FPS) to write a statement as follows:

_____,
Condition Statement

How might we _____ so that
                    (Key verb phrase)

_____, _____
(What will happen)   (Parameters)

Example: Because the eating habits of young people are causing health problems for them, we might determine a way to encourage children and teenagers to make better choices about food so that we will save lives and health dollars for the future generation of adults.

Step III: **Brainstorm** to determine at least five viable solutions that address the "Underlying Challenge." Include who, what, when, where, and how if possible.

Example: All of the following would be implemented within the next 5 years:

Solution #1. Education leaders could make sure healthy eating is focused on in at least one elementary grade, one middle school core academic class, and one high school core academic class.

Solution #2. The federal government could regulate the media's involvement in advertising unhealthy foods.

Solution #3. Community groups could pressure grocery stores to limit the unhealthy foods selection by refusing to buy certain unhealthy products.

Solution #4. Students could get a grant to pay for an advertising campaign to be distributed nationally on television, radio, and in print media. This campaign would provide information to young people and their parents that would challenge them to make better decisions about the foods they buy and their eating habits.

Solution #5. National PTA leaders could devise a plan for encouraging parents to stop buying unhealthy foods.

Step IV: This is one of the most important steps. Students brainstorm **criteria** with which to evaluate each of the five solutions. Criteria should be developed to include only a single dimension, should include the degree to which something will be evaluated, and should include the desired direction. Students should determine at least five criteria.

Example:

Criteria #1: Which solution would cost the least amount money?

Criteria #2: Which solution would take the least amount of time?

Criteria #3: Which solution would have the fewest barriers?

Criteria #4: Which solution would take the fewest people to implement?

Criteria #5: Which solution could be the most creative?

Step V: See the grid example: List the five solutions on the left side of the grid. List the five criteria across the top of the grid. Use only their numbers to save space. Rank each solution between one and five (one being lowest and five being highest). Each person could evaluate each solution individually and then discuss answers in order to reach consensus (i.e., everyone agrees), or everyone in the group could work together to determine the rank order. After all solutions have been given rank order numbers, add up the numbers and fill in the totals. The solution with the most points should be implemented. If there is a tie, go back and discuss until you have selected the best solution.

Criteria Ranking

Solutions	Criteria 1	Criteria 2	Criteria 3	Criteria 4	Criteria 5	Totals
Solution #1: Education leaders…	2	2	2	2	2	10
Solution #2: Federal government…	1	1	1	1	1	5
Solution #3: Community groups…	5	4	4	4	4	21
Solution #4: Kids could…	3	5	5	5	5	23
Solution #5: National PTA leaders…	4	3	3	3	3	16

Step VI: Create a "step-by-step" plan for implementation of the solution that received the highest score. The statement should answer in detail: who, what, when, where, and how; and it must clearly address the underlying problem.

Scenario Writing

This assessment strategy, which can be used across content areas, gives students an outlet for creativity (gfifted students especially enjoy writing scenarios). You can find many sources for scenario writing contests and example of scenarios on line. Here are the basic steps:

- ◆ Step 1: Decide what goals or objectives that address specific concepts and skills you plan to teach by using this strategy.

- ◆ Step 2: Tell students they will be writing a futuristic science fiction story. (If students are not sure of the genre, science fiction, review the subject or introduce it and make them clear before starting this product.)

Here is a possible activity to get students ready to write.

1. Divide students in to groups of four or five.

2. Give each student the same short science fiction story to read.

3. Hand out the following graphic organizer and ask each student to fill it out as he/she reads:

How do you know the setting is in the future?	Who are the important characters in the story?	What futuristic technology is used in the story?	List the words that indicate the story is futuristic	What is the main problem in the story?

4. Students should discuss their findings with each other and save the graphic organizer to help them write their own scenario.

♦ Step 3: Hand out a set of guidelines and scoring procedures. Review these with students so that they clearly understand what is expected of them.

Sample Guidelines:
Scenario Writing Assignment

Product to be turned in: A science-fiction story in which interesting characters solve a believable problem.

Due Date:_____

Criteria:
- Page limit—five (typed and double spaced, if possible)
- Setting must be at least 20 years in the future
- Characters must be interesting and believable
- Story must clearly show the elements of plot: basic situation (setting and characters), rising action (conflict/problem), climax (the problem is solved), and resolution (what happens after the problem is solved).
- Story must include use of futuristic technology
- Should include some futuristic vocabulary (these can be created words or words already associated with science fiction)
- Problem and solution must be clearly evident and realistic based on the created setting and characters
- Story must show understanding of content from this unit of study
- It is preferable if the story shows humanistic solutions.

Author note: Students and/or teacher should determine evaluation criteria for scoring the product.

Performance-Based Assessment

A culminating event or a performance that asks students to demonstrate their understanding of the concepts of a unit of study and their skills associated with that unit is another excellent method of assessing students' learning. The GRASPS method by Wiggins and McTighe is an excellent template for designing a performance assessment piece. The 4-Mat template is also an excellent method (see Chapter 3).

G.R.A.S.P.S (Goal, Role, Audience, Situation, Product or Performance, Standards) Sample Template

Goal	The goal is to write and perform an entertaining futuristic version of Shakespeare's A Midsummer Night's Dream.
Role	You are a member of the writing team and a cast member.
Audience	The teacher, your classmates, and if the play is good enough, the audience could be extended to include other classes or the whole school.
Situation	You must familiarize yourself with the entire play so that you can accurately reflect the themes, setting, characters, action, and Shakespeare's style. You must also be creative about using futuristic vocabulary and technology appropriately. Each team will write a scene and then the whole class will determine how to fit the scenes together to make the entire play.
Product or Performance	The product will be the written play. The play will also be performed.
Standards	The play must meet the following standards: ♦ It must accurately reflect A Midsummer Night's Dream, ♦ It must be convincingly futuristic, ♦ It must engage the audience.

Affective Domain Assessment

According to brain-based research, students learn more if they are engaged emotionally in a learning activity; therefore, it is important to determine how students are "feeling" about a topic of study and how they are learning about that topic. Using Journaling or Learning Logs can help teachers assess how affectively engaged their students are so that they might adjust instruction if necessary. These logs also help students learn how to think and write reflectively so that they can identify and record how they are feeling about what and how they are learning. Being able to clearly reflect about learning could facilitate students' taking responsibility for their own learning, and also encourage them to advocate for themselves as learners.

Journaling and Learning Logs

One of the best ways to assess the affective domain of students' learning about a unit of study is to ask them to write reflectively about that unit in a Journal or Learning Log.

Take the following steps to implement Learning Logs into your classroom:

- ◆ Step 1: Discuss reflective writing with your students. Tell them it is about verbalizing thoughts and feelings through writing. If your students have had no experience with reflective writing, you may need to model it for them by writing a short reflection from your own experience with a topic.

- ◆ Step 2: Tell students that they should keep a Learning Log in a special section of their notebook or use a special journaling notebook. Emphasize the importance of reflecting about what they are learning on a regular basis, and that they are evaluating how much they have learned or not learned, so that they can work toward maximizing learning.

- ◆ Step 3: Give students 2 to 10 minutes to write in their logs or journals at least twice per week. Make the time spent writing about learning an important activity. Emphasize that this kind of writing is informal and nonthreatening. Let students know you will read those logs on a regular basis and respond to what students have written when possible.

- ◆ Step 4: Make Learning Logs and journals an important assessment tool in your classroom. Adjust teaching if necessary based on what students write about in their logs.

Other uses for Learning Logs:

- • Reflecting on a unit of study to review for a test.

- • Explaining how learning has changed ideas or misconceptions.

- • Clarifying issues, especially if they are confusing.

- • Summarizing ideas

- • Previewing or predicting what will be presented next

- • Recording data from experiential activities

From (Fulwiler, 1980) and (Santa & Havens, 1991)

Self-Assessment and Peer Assessment

It is important to ask students to evaluate their own work and the work of other students. Students take responsibility for their learning and relieve the teacher of some of that responsibility when they evaluate (with criteria) their own work or the work of others. It is important in many cases that the teacher provides the criteria for the assessment, or that they guide the students to determine criteria. Assessment without criteria can be useless. Portfolio assessment and group work are two important methods of self- and peer assessment.

Portfolio Self-Assessment (Yancey, 1992)

Students' writing (which includes writing across contents) can best be assessed if students keep all of their work and present it in a portfolio (folder or notebook) to be evaluated in various ways including self-evaluation. Students should be encouraged to keep all of their drafts from the beginning of the year until the end. Teachers can ask students to reflect upon or set goals about their writing at the beginning of the year, at midyear, and at the end of the year. They could be asked to select best examples of their various types of writing. Here are some questions teachers could have students answer about their work.

- ♦ At the beginning
  - What are your strengths as a writer?
  - What are your weaknesses as a writer?
  - What kind of writing do you do best?
  - What kind of writing is more of a challenge for you?
  - What goals would you like to accomplish as a writer this year?
- ♦ At mid year:
  - What has changed about your writing so far?
  - What have you learned about yourself as a writer?
  - Do you need to adjust your goals at this point?
  - What do you know now that you didn't know before?
- ♦ At the end of the year:

Choose three to five pieces of writing for the teacher to evaluate. Answer the following questions about each piece:

- How does this piece of writing show what you have learned this year?

- Why is this a good example of your skills as a writer?

- Why did you choose this piece of writing?

- If you revised this piece, what would you do?

- What kinds of writing would you like to do more of?

Peer Assessment

Peer editing can be an excellent method of assessing students' writing. Here is a step-by- step guide to group or partner/peer editing:

Peer Editing—Argumentative Essay

♦ Step 1: Form groups of four or less or join a partner.

♦ Step 2: Number off if in a group or assign A and B to partners.

♦ Step 3: Teacher or students determine who goes first and in what order (i.e., number one or A do not necessarily go first).

♦ Step 4: First person reads his/her essay aloud to the group or to a partner.

♦ Step 5: The reader then asks these questions using the PQP method (Praise, Question, Perfect):

- What did you like best about my paper? (**P**)

- What questions do you have about my paper? (**Q**)

- What could I do to make my paper better? (**P**)

The person asking the questions should allow time for each member of the group or his/her partner to make a specific response to each question.

Author note: The teacher may need to model appropriate responses to questions about writing, and students may need to practice responding appropriately.

This step is repeated until all members or the group or both partners have read.

♦ Step 6: Pass the papers to the right or exchange papers.

♦ Step 7: Each person reads another person's paper for the purpose of giving feedback that is structured by the following analytical rubric:

Organization	Focus	Support/Data	Style	Conventions
High Score 4				
Advances ideas by using IBC (Introduction, Body, Conclusion) form with appropriate paragraphing and smooth transitions.	One main idea or claim that is advanced through use of related sub-ideas.	Sufficient, relevant, and reasonable details that include examples and other forms of elaboration. Includes a warrant that draws important conclusions about that data.	Sophisticated use of syntax and diction appropriate to the purpose and audience.	No more than three errors in Grammar, Usage, Mechanics, and Spelling (GUMS).
Acceptable Score 3				
Advances ideas by using IBC form with appropriate paragraphing and transitions. Shows some weaknesses in transitions or content of easy parts.	Slight loss of focus at times. Gets off topic occasionally.	Sufficient data that is usually relevant and reasonable, but failure to draw high-level conclusions.	Diction and syntax show some lack of sophistication. Not always aligned with audience and purpose.	Has more than three errors that slightly decrease readability of text.
Low Score 2				
Fails to use IBC form appropriately and shows significant weaknesses in use of transitions.	Often gets off topic. Includes too many unrelated ideas.	Insufficient, irrelevant, and irrational data used to support claims.	Weak use of language and sentence structure. Word choice and sentence structure lack complexity and variety. Weak sense of audience and purpose.	Errors in grammar, usage, mechanics, and spelling significantly reduce readability.
Criteria Totals				

Students are encouraged to keep the scores broken into criteria rather than averaging scores; however, the process should give students a sense of whether they are performing at a high, acceptable, or low level on the paper holistically.

Or for middle school or less sophisticated students, they could answer a series of questions as follows:

Check ___Yes or ___No. If the answer is no, please answer the second part of the question.

Yes   No

___   ___   1.   Is this paper in IBC form? If not, what is missing or poorly developed?

___   ___   2.   Does this paper successfully use transitions? If not, circle the transitions and note any places where a transition is needed.

___   ___   3.   Is the main idea of this paper stated clearly? If not, what is the problem?

___   ___   4.   Do sub-ideas support the main idea in order to advance the claim? If not, what questions do you have?

___   ___   5.   Does the writer include enough relevant and reasonable data to support his/her claims? If not, what is missing?

___   ___   6.   Does the writer draw interesting and reasonable conclusions (the warrant) about his/her data? If not, where is a warrant needed?

___   ___   7.   Does the writer use sophisticated language? If not, which words are worn out or less useful?

___   ___   8.   Does the writer use varied and complex sentence structure where appropriate? If not, what is the general pattern of the sentences?

___   ___   9.   Does the writer's style address the audience appropriately? If not, what word choices indicate inappropriateness?

___   ___   10.   Does the writer's style maintain the purpose of argumentation to advance the claim? If not, what does he/she do instead?

♦ Step 8: After peers have completed the analytical rubric or questions, they may provide editing help by identifying any grammar, usage, mechanics, or spelling errors they see in the paper.

♦ Step 9: Students should return each writer's paper and their evaluation of that paper, including comments and the scores they determined from the rubric. Teachers could also grade peer-editing efforts.

♦ Step 10: Students are encouraged to revise papers prior to submitting them for a grade or for feedback from the teacher.

Assessment Tools

Beyond the quantitative assessment of marking right answers on a multiple choice, true/false, short answer, matching, or other convergent method, there are three tools that are invaluable for qualitative or quantitative analysis of products that are more divergent in nature. The three methods are:

Check List (Also a Quantitative Tool)

A checklist is an easy way to determine if students have included all the aspects of the assessment product when they turn it in to the teacher. Students should have access to the list so that they will know exactly what is expected from them. Parts of the assignment as well as qualitative requirements may be listed. Teachers can assign points to each aspect of the assignment that is included. Each check can mean the same or different points. If points are used, the total should be 100 in most cases. See the sample Checklist:

Generic Research Paper Checklist

___ Title page (Neat, organized, balanced, creative, evidence of abstract thinking)
  ___ Exceptional (5 points)
  ___ Above Average (4 points)
  ___ Average (3 points)
  ___ Below Average (2 points)
  ___ Well-below Average (1 point)
  ___ No title page (0 points)
___Works Cited page (Correct form)
  ___ 5 sources in correct form (10 points)
  ___ 4 sources in correct form (8 points)
  ___ 3 sources in correct form (6 points)
  ___ 2 sources in correct form (4 points)
  ___ Less than 2 sources (no credit)
  ___ Sources not in correct form (no credit for each one that is incorrect)
___ Parenthetical Documentation (Correct form)
  ___ Used correctly to give credit for paraphrasing and direct quotes (20 points)
  ___ Incorrect form and usage (no credit)
  ___ Plagiarism (paper receives a zero)
___ Thesis Statement (Sufficiently narrow and proved by data)
  ___ Engaging, appropriately narrow, proved by the data presented (15 points)
  ___ Some weaknesses, but proved by the data (12 points)
  ___ Some weaknesses, some weaknesses in supportive data (10 points)
  ___ Inappropriate thesis statement, not proved (5 points)
  ___ No thesis statement (0 points)
___ Supportive Data
  ___ Relevant, interesting, accurate, sufficient (20 points)
  ___ Some weaknesses (18)
  ___ Acceptable (15)
  ___ Very poor (5)
___Warrant (Evidence of synthesis)
  ___ Evidence of high level of synthesis of information (20 points)
  ___ Some evidence of synthesis (18)
  ___ Acceptable evidence of synthesis (15)
  ___ No evidence of synthesis (0)
___ Conventions
  ___ No more than 3 errors (10 points)
  ___ 3 to 10 errors (5 points)
  ___ More than 10 errors (no points)

_____ Total Points Earned

Product Guide

Students should know as much as possible about what is expected of them. A product guide can provide the parameters for assignments. See the following Sample Product Guide:

Product Guide for Multiple Intelligences Projects/Products

Intelligence	Product	Parts	Attributes
Linguistic	Essay	Introduction	Interesting and states the main idea.
		Body	Paragraphs begin with a topic sentence that reflects a main idea. Main ideas are well supported with logical details. Writer uses transitions to make the paragraphs coherent.
		Conclusion	Contains no new main ideas. Brings the ideas to a close gracefully.
		Content	Must have unity, be logical, and should sufficiently cover the topic.
		Mechanics	Grammar, usage, mechanics, and spelling must not interfere significantly with a reader's ability to understand the essay.
	Oral Presentation (Individual)	Written copy	Must include the above attributes.
		Introduction	Introduce the topic to grab the audience's attention and make the main idea clear.
		Content	Sequence key points with smooth transitions, adhere to time limit, and involve the audience appropriately.
		Summary	Review key points, answer questions from the audience, and include a closing statement.
		Visual Aids	Highlight key points, write content boldly enough for everyone to see, and show quality work.
		Use of Visual Aids	Use during presentation to enhance content, hold still and at eye level, and display long enough for all to see.
		Voice	Speak clearly, use Standard English, and enunciate using sufficient volume.
		Body Language	Make appropriate eye contact with the audience, use formal posture, don't fidget, and use natural movements and gestures.
	Group Oral Presentation	Same parts as above	Make sure all students share equally in presenting to the class.

Intelligence	Product	Parts	Attributes
Spatial	Visual Arts	Title	Write the title unobtrusively on the back of the work or on a separate piece of paper.
		Two- to three-dimensional piece of art work	Supportive of key elements of the topic, aesthetically pleasing and complete.
		Commentary	Explain how the artwork addresses the requirements of the assignment.
	Poster	Title	Prominent, concise, legible, bold print, describes the topic, attention getting.
		Illustrations	Neat, supportive of key elements of assignment, colorful, and complete.
		Text	Legible, printed, grammatically correct, and matches the purpose of the product.
		Space	Balanced, uncluttered, compact, and uniform.

Intelligence	Product	Parts	Attributes
Kinesthetic	Drama (Live)	Script	Must be written in drama form (i.e. acts, scenes, cast of characters, stage directions, etc.).
		Introductions	Share title of presentation, introduce each member, explain each member's role in the performance.
		Content	Accurate, if a dramatization of a text. Follows an interesting storyline including exposition, rising action, climax, and resolution.
		Voice	Paced delivery, appropriate volume, clear enunciation of words.
		Body Language	Eyes focused appropriately for a drama, appropriate posture, appropriate facial expressions, appropriate gestures, movements clearly seen by the audience. No fidgeting or misbehaving.
		Props	Appropriate costuming and sets that support the action in the play.
		Credits	List contributions of members at the end of the performance.
	Drama (video)	Same as above	Add: Smooth transitions between scenes, clear images, and actors' lines clearly audible.
	Dance Performance	Written commentary	Must clearly explain the purposes of the movements as they are related to the assignment.
		Performance of dance	Appropriate accompaniment, meaningful use of choreography to convey meaning associated with the assignment, meets time limit, aesthetically pleasing. High level of abstraction, symbolism.
	Board Games	Title	Prominent, legible, supports theme, concise, creative, original, neat.
		Objective	Clearly stated within the directions, factual, and incorporates skill.
		Directions and rules	Clear, sequenced, neatly printed, and includes criteria for winning.
		Game board	Clearly labeled, bold print, poster board size, and illustrated creatively.
		Game pieces	Durable and manageable size.
		Packaging	Attractive, colorful, functional, credits.
	Puppet Show	Presentation	See drama for specifics on presentation.
		Puppets	Well-constructed, aesthetically pleasing, accurate.

Intelligence	Product	Parts	Attributes
Musical	Original Song or Score	Written song or score	Must reflect the key elements of the assignment. Meaningful use of lyrics and/or melody to convey ideas. Original lyrics and/or score.
		Performance of song or score	Appropriate volume and clarity. Aesthetically pleasing. High level of abstraction, symbolism. Meets time limits.
		Commentary	Must explain how the song or score reflects key elements of the assignment.
Logical/ Mathematical	Graphs, Charts or Graphic Organizers	Title	Describes the topic, is neat, and legible. Supports theme, concise, creative, original.
		Text	Legible, grammatically and mathematically correct, and matches the purpose of the assignment.
		Space	Balanced, uncluttered, compact, uniform.
		Graphics	Neat, supportive of data, complete and accurate.
	Games and Puzzles	Title	Describes the topic, neat and legible. Supports theme, concise, creative, and original.
		Directions and rules	Neatly printed, grammatically correct, and match the purpose of the assignment. Objectives clearly stated. Incorporates skill. Clearly stated rules, sequenced, criteria for succeeding.
		Graphics	Neat, creative, aesthetically pleasing, original, or original layout of published graphics.

Rubric (Holistic or Analytical Measures)

A holistic rubric is a summative evaluation of a product or performance. The evaluator gives the product or performance a number or level of achievement based on how the product or performance matches a description of the features of that score. Example of a holistic rubric:

Holistic Rubric for Oral Presentations

Distinguished—4

- Introduction clearly grabs the audience's attention and shows evidence of excellent organization.
- Excellent choice of points that are well-sequenced.
- Powerful conclusion that summarizes and influences the audience in some way.

- Adheres to time limit—not too long or too short.
- Excellent presence with the audience.
- Excellent eye contact and body language. Excellent enunciation and volume.

Above Average—3

- Introduction interesting and shows evidence of organization.
- Good choice of points that are sequenced.
- Very good conclusion that summarizes and has some effect on the audience.

- Adheres to time limit or only slightly over or under the time limit.
- Very good presence with the audience.
- Very good eye contact and body language.
- Very good enunciation and volume.

Satisfactory—2

- Introduction shows an attempt to get audience's attention and evidence of some organization.
- Some good points, but not always sequenced for the best effect.
- Satisfactory conclusion that summarizes main points.

- Not quite long enough.
- Acceptable presence with the audience.
- Very little distracting body language.
- Usually audible and some problems with clear enunciation of words.

Unsatisfactory—1

- No attempt to engage the audience and information confusion.
- May misbehave or refuse to participate appropriately.
- Points confusing and weak. Out of sequence or disorganized in general.
- Conclusion weak or left out.

- Too short.
- Out of touch with the audience. Fidgeting and other distracting movements.
- Hard to hear and understand.
- Key words mispronounced.

One can change a holistic rubric into an analytical rubric, by giving points to parts of the product that are separated in the discrete criteria. In the case of an analytical rubric, the evaluator does not give a total score, but gives separate scores for criteria. The analytical rubric is useful for formative evaluation or feedback to the student.

Here is an example of an Analytical Rubric to help you rate yourself in terms of your ability to successfully differentiate a lesson.

Lesson Differentiation Observation Rubric

Meeting Students' Needs	Method/ Model	Engagement	Standards	Assessment
Level—Sophisticated Score 4				
Lesson design consistently matches the students' needs based on an assessment of readiness learning style, and interests.	Time on task 90%–100% with excellent transitions.	Lesson design closely matches students' affective and cognitive domains.	Activities based on goals and standards consistently challenge each student to use the highest order thinking ability they can.	Acceptable evidence of deep and enduring understanding authentically addressed through cognitive and affective domains.
Level—Competent Score 3				
Lesson design often matches students needs based on assessment of readiness, learning style, and interests.	Time on task 80%–89% with good transitions.	Lesson design often matches students' affective and cognitive domains.	Activities based on goals and standards often challenge each student to use the highest order thinking ability he/she can.	Evidence consistently reflects students' level of achievement on skills and knowledge embedded in the curriculum standards.
Level—Adequate Score 2				
Lesson design matches most, but not all students' needs based on readiness, learning styles, and interests.	Time on task 70%–79% with adequate transitions.	Lesson design at times matches students' affective and cognitive domains.	Activities based on goals and standards sometimes challenge students to use higher order thinking ability.	Evidence adequately reflects students' level of achievement on skills and knowledge embedded in curriculum standards.
Level—Perfecting Score 1				
Lesson design inconsistently matches students' readiness, learning styles, and interests.	Time on task below 70% with some rough transitions.	Lesson design inconsistently matched students' affective and cognitive domains.	Activities somewhat aligned with goals and standards often miss chances to take students to higher levels of thinking.	Evidence inconsistently reflects students' level of achievement on skills and knowledge embedded in curriculum standards.
Scores on each criteria				

Summary

Assessing what students know and are able to do can be thrilling and validating to teachers who are committed to making those assessments meaningful for their students. Standardized tests can give us a great deal of useful information especially when they are used to show trends in large groups and to help improve educational opportunities of all students. They should never be used to punish or demean anyone. Students are delighted when they do well on any assessment, and most students have come to believe that their value is associated with how well they do when they are evaluated. Classroom teachers must help students learn to use all kinds of assessments to help them grow as people. They should make assessment procedures as fair and helpful as possible, so that all students can know how well they are performing and where they are in relation to their own learning journey, and how well they compare with their peers.

As you can see from the many strategies detailed in this chapter, the assessment process can be as instructive as a teacher's direct instruction. Most constructivists believe that students only learn when they ask questions and struggle with problems to find reasonable solutions. Whatever you believe about how students learn, you should use differentiated assessment strategies in order to fully understand what all of your students know and are able to do.

5

Putting it All Together

This chapter presents some general guidelines for using the many strategies and concepts for differentiating instruction to meet students' needs that were presented in earlier chapters.

General Guidelines

When planning a unit some **general steps** are recommended for any secondary lesson or unit design. Work backwards from what you want all students to understand and be able to do. If you do not begin with the end in mind, you may not get what you are after in the form of students' learning. There are several issues to consider as you plan what you want students to know and to be able to do in your content area. These are:

Step 1: What Will Students Learn?

History and Science

To begin planning a unit for high content areas like History and Science, use what Wiggins and McTighe (1998) call a "3-Circle Audit" (three concentric circles). This is an important step when planning to differentiate because the most challenged and unmotivated students may only be able to succeed in learning a limited amount of the content, and some of them may also lack important skills to respond successfully to large amounts of content. In addition, more advanced and motivated students may require more content in order to feel challenged.

A "Three-Circle Audit" looks like this graphically:

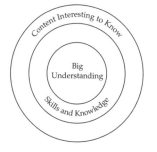

Three-Circle Audit

1. In the middle of a circle, put the critical understanding or understandings (not a big number) students should gain from your unit. This understanding should be based primarily on curriculum standards determined by your school system.
    Rule of thumb: *This is what you want students to remember for as long as they live.*

2. Place in the next outer circle, the critical concepts, skills, and knowledge that make up the "bare bones" of the subject area. In other words, what information is critical for students to know, understand, and be able to do to meet teachers' and school systems' standards for evidence of accomplishment in the subject area. (This circle is for everyone, but some students may already know some of this information and these skills; therefore they may be able to move to the third circle)

3. In the outer-most circle, place the information with which students should become familiar.

You may also use the Three-Circle Audit for other subjects; however, here are some specific suggestions for Math and English/Language Arts.

Math

For each Math unit, determine the discrete math concepts and skills students must master to show they understand those concepts and can perform those skills in the context of word problems for the level of math you are teaching. (This is for everyone.)

To enrich math, add the skill of using multiple math concepts and skills in real world applications and for more abstract applications. (This is for the most advanced and motivated learners.) Use pre-assessment and post-assessment for evidence of mastery in order to differentiate product, process, and content for all students.

English/Language Arts

English is more skill-based than content based. Focus on discrete reading comprehension skills, critical reading skills, and writing skills in the context of print and nonprint selections. The goal of English/Language Arts is for students to gain lifelong literacy (reading and writing) for their work and for their pleasure.

Helpful Hints:

- Use a spiraling approach whereby skills are revisited in various levels of emphasis in a variety of literacy experiences.

- Everyone should have practice until mastery in basic reading comprehension skills such as: determining main idea, understanding how details work together to support main ideas, determining the meanings of words in context, understanding the relationships among words and concepts (analogies), being able to make inferences and draw conclusions, comparing and contrasting, determining cause and effect, and understanding how writing is sequenced.

- As students move from lower grades to higher grades, reading comprehension becomes less important, and critical reading takes its place. Critical reading includes: determining author's tone, and attitude and how these create the mood of a literary work, determining how symbolism reveals information about a literary work, understanding how figurative language works to create understanding and imagery in a literary work, determining the themes and psychological effect of a literary work, and, in general, analyzing the impact of an author's style.

- To differentiate English/Language Arts, consider where each student is in his/her ability to comprehend and critically read a wide variety of reading materials.

- Differentiate reading materials, oral and written questions, and writing assignments based on students' level of literacy.

- Let students choose as much as possible the level of reading selections and the method in which they will demonstrate competency with that material.

Step 2: How Will You Determine Acceptable Evidence?

After determining what students will learn from the unit, decide how to evaluate if they have learned what you have taught them. This is a good place to plan how to differentiate for students in order to determine a fair assessment of what they know (Differentiating the Product.)

Helpful Hints:

- Giving choices is a critical concept to keep in mind when planning assessment that is fair and that accurately determines what students know and are able to do in a given area.

- Assessing the affective domain is essential to determine holistic learning.

- Problem solving authentic or real world projects are excellent methods for determining if meaningful learning has taken place.

- Aligning teacher-made assessments with any required standardized tests will help students achieve in today's high stakes, accountability-based educational systems.

Step 3: What Differentiated Activities Will Maximize Learning for *All* Students?

Plan whole class and differentiated learning activities that will meet the needs of all students.

Planning Unit Activities

1. **Beginning a unit or lesson**: For the beginning of any unit, plan an activity that will engage all learners.

   Helpful Hints:

   - Think about what you know about the human growth and development of adolescents. You should know that they are highly egocentric, and that what their peers think of them is critical.

   - Think of activities that ask them to focus on themselves in relationship to a topic.

   - Give them chances to go before the class, to move, and to laugh (i.e., engage them affectively).

   - Show them the importance of the topic or theme in terms of real world application.

   - Help them see that they can be interested and successful as they work on the unit.

2. **Collecting new information**: Collect new information to add to the baseline information you gathered at the beginning of the school year. Remember that information about students is not static. Students have

remarkable potential for having spurts of ability and motivation to learn certain topics. However, you should probably have a general idea about each of your students' reading levels, interests, and learning styles.

Use a method such as pretest or quiz, interactive discussion, or KWL (**K** = what students know, **W** = what students want to learn, **L** = what students learned) brainstorming to gather information on what students already know about a topic or theme.

Because you already have a fairly good idea about your students needs, you should have a good idea about which differentiation method will best align with those needs in order to accomplish your goals for the unit or lesson.

3. **Planning Differentiated Activities (Differentiating the process)**:

   Helpful Hints on how to select an appropriate process of differentiation:

   ◆ **Group Work**: All middle school students love group work; therefore, you should consider using at least one grouping strategy per unit. Three levels of difficulty will suffice. Most high school students enjoy group work also; however, because grade point averages (GPA) are so critical in high school, avoid giving group grades that could negatively affect a students' GPA.

   ◆ **Whole Class**: Present information that will interest the whole class, and then tier activities for at least three levels of difficulty, several types of interests, or the three major learning channels: visual, auditory, and tactile/kinesthetic.

   ◆ **Individualizing**: If you have less than four students whose needs differ from the majority of the class, consider contracting, compacting, independent study, or apprenticeship.

   ◆ **Special Considerations**: If you have students who do poorly when given too much freedom, consider activities that will limit choices and activities during which the whole class moves.

   ◆ Within a standard routine, vary your learning experiences. You may want to use a different strategy with each unit, and then revisit those to which your students best responded.

   ◆ Consider that certain students are uncomfortable with open-ended problem-solving activities and others thrive on it. Do not frustrate or turn off either group by mismatching the activity with their needs.

   ◆ When you use projects that engage students' multiple intelligences, plan activities that allow students to learn through their strength and demonstrate mastery through that strength. For instance, if a student has an arts intelligence (i.e., music, spatial (visual arts), kinesthetic (dance)), have him/her use that art in order to remember concepts or procedures in core academic subjects. Have student apply those skills and knowledge to real world arts problems as often as possible. Collaborate with arts elective teachers to help in determining problems that students would use their arts intelligence to solve. For example: If a student has musical intelligence, have him/her learn math concepts by singing or playing songs or rhythms. Have the student demonstrate understanding of the math concept by solving a real world music problem that requires understanding of a discrete math concept.

Step 4: What Materials Will You Need to Teach the Lesson?

The next step can be a matter of creating and locating materials, such as textbooks, overhead instructions, handouts, technology resources, and arts materials. Some teachers need to think about this step earlier because they may be limited by the available materials.

Helpful Hints: You need to know the following:

- How well does each student read?
- How much computer access will you have for your unit?
- What other media sources are available?
- What can your textbook and its ancillary materials add to your unit?
- What community resources are available?
- What other resources are available in your school and from the homes of your students?
- What arts resources do you have for creative activities? (Author note: You should also discern what capability your students have in their homes for doing arts-based projects. Some families are not set up to purchase arts materials.)

Step 5: How Will You Present the Lesson to the Students and in What Order?

Finally, determine how you will present the lesson to the students. Generally, a six-step lesson seems to be the best plan, although I do not always follow that plan in the lessons presented in this chapter. The following is a good outline to follow:

- **Starter**: One of the main purposes of a beginning activity is to help students focus on a topic. This can be achieved through any of the following:
  - An exciting hook to get students interested in a topic
  - A KWL chart to stimulate access prior knowledge of a topic
  - A five-question or other number of questions quiz (just so it is short) to help students review and to help you know how much students are learning
  - A journal assignment related to the topic
- **Review**: This can be associated with the starter or warm-up, especially if you use a quiz about the prior class.
- **Instruction:** This is where the goals and objectives of the lesson are presented with an explanation of new concepts or a guide through new information. Generally, this is whole class instruction.
- **Guided practice**: This is the part of the lesson where most differentiation of content and process occurs.
- **Independent practice:** This can be in-class work, homework practice, or projects. During independent practice students may choose differentiated product assignments.
- **Wrap-up**: Review the material from this lesson and/or anticipate the next lesson. Choose from among the following ideas to end the lesson:
  - Allow students to share their work
  - Use a Think-Pair-Share Activity (Ask students to think about what they learned today, find a partner, and share their ideas with that partner).
  - Have students write a paragraph about what they learned, how they feel about it, and how they might use that knowledge. This paragraph could be a "ticket out of the room."
  - Go back to the KWL chart and record as a class what they learned today.
  - Play a game (like Around the World) in which one student stands up, goes to the desk of another student to challenge him/her. The teacher poses a question. The student who answers it either stays standing or the student who was seated stands up. Students continue challenging each other until the bell rings.

References

A personal tour of multiple intelligences. (1994). Seattle, Washington: Citizens Education Center.

Altshuler, G., & Williams, A. Jr. (1988). *Creativity as an Exact Science.* New York: Gordon and Breach.

Ammon, B. D., & Sherman, G. W. (1996). *Worth a thousand words: An annotated guide to picture books for older readers.* Libraries Unlimited.

Anderson, L., & Krathwohl, D. R., et al. (2000). *A Taxonomy of Learning, Teaching, and Assessing: A Revision of Bloom's Taxonomy of Educational Objectives.* Harlow, UK: Longman Publishing Group.

Armstrong, T. (1994). *Multiple intelligences in the classroom.* Alexandria, VA: Association for Supervision and Curriculum Development.

Armstrong, T. (1993). *Seven kinds of smart: Identifying and developing your many intelligences.* New York: Plume, Penguin Group.

Atwell, N. (1987). *In the middle: Writing, reading and learning with adolescents.* Portsmouth, NH: Boyton/Cook Publishers.

ASIT, a revolutionary creative thinking method: Will lead you step-by-step from deadlock to breakthroughs. Retrieved June 4, 2004, from www.Start2Learn.com

Assessment Alternative in Mathematics, a booklet from the California Mathematics Council and EQUAL.

Banks, J. (1997). *Educating citizens in a multicultural society.* New York: Teachers College Press.

Barrett, S. R. (1992). *It's all in your head: A guide to understanding your brain and boosting your brain power.* Minneapolis, MN: Free Spirit Publishing, Inc.

Barton, M. L. & Heidemic, C. (2002). *Teaching reading in mathematics.* Aurora, CO: Mid-Continent Regional Educational Laboratory (MCREL).

Benjamin, A. (2002). *Differentiated instruction: A guide for middle and high school teachers.* Larchmont, NY: Eye on Education.

Billmeyer, R., & Barton, M. L. (1998). *Teaching reading in the content area.* Aurora, CO: Mid-Continent Regional Educational Laboratory (MCREL).

Blosser, P. E. (1973). *Handbook of effective questioning techniques.* Worthington, OH: Education Associates.

Bloom, B., Englehart, M., Furt, E., Hill, W., Krathwhol, D. (1956). Taxonomy of Educational Objectives Handbook I: Cognitive domain. New York: Longmans Green.

Brain Gym Exercises. Retrieved May 16, 2004, from http://esl.about.com/library/lessons/blbraingym.htm

Brain Gym International. Retrieved May 8, 2004, from http://www.braingym.org

Bruner, J., Goodnow, J. J., & Austin, G. A. (1967), *A study of thinking.* New York: Science Editions.

Bono, E. de. (1985). *Six thinking hats.* Boston: Back Bay Books.

Butler, K. A. (1987) Successful learning strategies for the emerging adolescent. *Oklahoma Middle Level Education Association Journal,* 1–7.

Idyllwild, C. H. Caine Learning: Brain/Mind Constructivism. Retrieved May 31, 2004, from http://caine learning.com

Center for Studies in Higher Order Literacy. Retrieved May 31, 2004, from University of Missouri Web site, http://members.aol.com/CSHOLUMK/home.htm

Chapman, C., Chapman, G., & Gayle, H. (2002). *Differentiated instructional strategies-one size doesn't fit all.* Thousand Oaks, CA: Corwin Press, Inc.

Chapman, A., (Ed.). (1993). *Making sense: Teaching critical reading across the curriculum.* New York: The College Board.

Cohen, E. (1986). *Designing Groupwork: Strategies for the Heterogeneous Classroom.* New Yori: Teachers College Press.

Costa, A., & Kallick B. (2000). *Habits of mind: Discovering and exploring.* VA: Association for Supervision and Curriculum.

Covey, S. Jr. (1998). *The seven habits of effective teens.* New York: Fireside.

Cunningham, P. M. (1978). Mumble reading for beginning readers. *The Reading Teacher, 31,* 409–411.

Daniels, H. (1994). *Literature circles: Voice and choice in the student-centered classroom.* Portland, ME: Stenhouse Publishers.

Designs for thinking. Retrieved May 29, 2004, from http://www.mapthemind.com

Dennison, P. E., & Dennison, G. E. (1986). *Brain gym.* Glendale, CA: Edu-Kinesthetics, Inc.

Eberle, R. (1996). Scamper On. Austin, TX: Prufrock Press.

Educational Sponge Activities. Retriefed August 29, 2004, from http://tepserver.ucsd.edu/courses/tep129/EductionalSponges.pdf

English: Learning area: SCAMPER. Retrieved June 1, 2004, from www.discover.tased.edu.au/english/scamper.htm

Erik Erikson's Eight stages of psychosocial development. Retrieved September 20, 2003, from Erikson Home Page, http://facultyweb.cortland.edu/~ANDERSMD /ERIK/welcome.html

Erikson, E. (1950). *Childhood and society.* New York: Norton.

EQI.Org. Retrieved May 23, 2004, from www.eqi.org

EQ.Org. Retrieved May 24, 2004, from www.eq.org

Felder, R., (1993). Reaching the second tier: Learning and teaching styles in college science education. *Journal of College Science Teaching, 23,* (4), 286–290.

Flow and Mihaly Csikszentmihaly. Retrieved June 1, 2004, from www.austega.com/education/articles/flow.htm

Ford, D. Y., & Harris III, J. J. (2000, September). A framework for infusing multicultural curriculum into gifted education. *Roper Review, 23,* (1), 4–10.

Ford-Harris matrix using Bloom-Banks framework (Concept: Social injustices-stereotypes and prejudice), from Ford & Harris, 1999, *Multicultural Gifted Education.* Retrieved December 15, 2003, from http://www.coe.ohio-state.edu/dyford/Lessonplans /ford-harris.matrix.htm

Frayer, D.A., Fredrick, W. C., & Klausmeier, H. G. (1969). *Technical report N. k16.* Milwaukee, WI: University of Wisconsin.

Fry, F. B. (1977, December). Readability graph: Clarification, validity and extensions to level 17. *Journal of Reading,* 249.

Fulwiler, T. (1980). Journals across the disciplines. *The English Journal, 69,* (9), 14–19.

Gardner, H. (1983). *Frames of mind: The theory of the multiple intelligences.* New York: Basic Books.

Gardner, H. (1993). *Multiple intelligences: The theory in practice.* New York: Basic Books.

Gallagher, S.A., (1997, Summer). Problem-based learning: Where did it come from, what does it do, and where is it going? *Journal for the Education of the Gifted, 20,* (4), 332–362.

Ginn, W. Y. (2003). Jean Piaget-Intellectual Development. Retrieved September 20, 2003, from http://www.sk.com.br/sk-piage.htm

Glazer, S. M. (1998). *Assessment IS instruction: Reading, writing, spelling and phonics for ALL learners.* Norwood, MA: Christopher Gordon Publishers, Inc.

Gorman, M., & Tennapel, D. (2002, August). What teens want: Thirty graphic novels you can't live without. *School Library Journal, 48,* (8), 42–47.

Gorman, M. (2003, November/December). Graphic novels and the curriculum connection. *Library Media Connection, 22,* (3), 20–21.

Gregorc, A. F., & Butler, K. A. (1984 April). Learning is a matter of style. *Vocational Education 59,* (3), 27–29.

Gregorc Associates, 1999–2004. Retrieved June 3, 2004, from http://www.gregroc.com

Hannaford, C. (1995). *Smart moves: Why learning is not all in your head.* Arlington, VA: Great Ocean Publishers.

Harmin, M. (1994). *Inspiring active learning: A handbook for teachers.* Alexandria, VA: Association for Supervision and Curriculum Development.

Hawthorne, N. (2000). *House of the Seven Gables.* New York: Barnes and Noble.

Hots: Higher-order thinking skills. Retrieved May 31, 2004, linked to REAP Control, University of Missouri Web site, from http://xnet.rrc.mb.ca/ glenh/hots.htm

How to brainstorm. Retrieved June 1, 2004, from www.ciadertising.org/studies/student/97_fall/pratitioner/osborn/afosborn.htm

How to use SCAMPER. Retrieved June 1, 2004, from www.brainstorming.co.uk/tutorials/scampertutorial.html

Humanmetrics: Jung typology test. Retrieved May 29, 2004, from http://www.humanmetrics.com/cgi-win/Jtypes1.htm

Hyerle, D. (2000). *A field guide to using visual tools.* Alexandria, VA: Association for Supervision and Curriculum Development (ASCD).

Innovative learning group: Thinking maps. Retrieved May 29, 2004, from www.thinking maps.com

Individual differences: The 4Mat system. Retrieved September 20, 2003, from http://chiron.valsta.edu/whuitt/col/instruct/4mat.htm

Introduction to Muds. Retrieved September 16, 2004, from http://www.mudconnect.com

Jago, C. (2000). *With rigor for all: Teaching the classics to contemporary students.* Portland, ME: Calendar Island Publishers.

Jensen, Eric. 1998. *Teaching with the Brain in Mind.* Alexandria, VA: Association for Supervision and Curriculum Development.

Jones, C. Creativity boosters. Retrieved June 1, 2004, from www.mca-i.org/members/m2m/m2m_02nov.htm

Joyce, B., & Weil, M. (1986). *Models of teaching.* Englewood Cliffs, NJ: Prentice-Hall, Inc.

Jung, C. (1933). Modern man in search of a soul. Orlando, FL: Harcourt.

Kagen, S. (1992). *Cooperative learning.* San Juan Capistrano, CA: Kagan Cooperative Learning.

Kaplan, S. Gould, B., & Siegel, V. (1995). *The flip book: A quick and easy method for developing differentiated learning experiences.* CA: Educator to Educator, Inc.

Keller, T. S. (1968). Good-bye teacher…. *Journal of Applied Behaviour Analysis, 5,* 79–89.

Kiersey, D. (1998). *Please understand me II: Temperament, character, intelligence.* Del Mar, CA: Prometheus Nemesis Book Company.

Kiersey Temperament Sorter II, Retrieved September 13, 2004, from http://www.advisor team.com

Kolb, D., (1984). *Experiential learning: Experience as the source of learning and development.* Englewood Cliffs, NJ: Prentice Hall.

Kulik, C. L, Kulik, J. A., & Bangert-Downs, R. L. (1990). Effectiveness mastery learning programs: A meta analysis. *Review of Educational Research 60,* 265–299.

Latta, D.K. "Graphic Novels and Trade Paperback (TPB) Reviews," Retrieved May 8, 2004, from http://www.geocities.com/SoHo/study/4273/graphic.htm

Learning styles and the 4Mat system: A cycle of learning. (2002). Retrieved June 18, 2003, from http://volcano.und.nodak.edu/vwdocs/msh/llc/is/4mat.html

Leppien, J. H. (2000, September). Web sites to help teachers create more challenging curriculum for gifted students. *Teaching for High Potential, II,* (2), 1–2.

Literature circles. Retrieved May 31, 2004, from www.literaturecircles.com

Literature circles resources center. Retrieved May 31, 2004, from http://fac-staff.seattleu. edu/kshlnoe/Litcircles

LogMOO. (2003). Retrieved October 25, 2003, from http://ahynes1.homeip.net:8000/moo

Maker, C. J., Nielson, A. B., & Rogers, J. A. (1994). Multiple intelligences: Giftedness, diversity and problem solving. *Teaching Exceptional Children, 27,* (1), 4–19.

Maker, J. (1996). *Nurturing giftedness in young children.* Arlington, VA: Council for Exceptional Children.

Malta, G. Puberty 101—Five stages of puberty, 2003. Puberty 101 Archives. Retrieved September 21, 2003, from http://www.puberty101.com/p_pubgirls.shtml and p_pub boys.shtml

Manzo, A., & Manzo, U. (1994). *Teaching children to be literate: A reflective approach.* Orlando, FL: Harcourt.

Mathematics: Applications and Connections: Course 3. (1999). Columbus: OH: Glencoe/ McGraw Hill.

McCarthy, B. (1981, 1982). *The 4Mat System: Teaching to learning styles with right/left mode techniques.* Wauconda, IL: About Learning.

Michalko, M. (1991). *A handbook of business creativity.* Berkeley, CA: Ten Speed Press.

Mind Maps. Retrieved June 4, 2004, from http:webits3.appstate.edu/apples/study/Creativity/new_page_19.htm

Myers, I. B., & McCaulley, M. H. (1985). *Manual: A guide to the development and uses of the Myers-Briggs Type Indicator.* Palo Alto, CA: Consulting Psychologists Press.

O'Brien, L. (1990). *Learning channels: Preference checklist.* Philadelphia: Research for Bette Schools.

O'Brien, L. (1989, October). Learning styles: Make the student aware. *National Association of Secondary School Principals (NASSP) Bulletin, 73,* (519), 85–89.

Osborne, A. F. (1953). *Applied imagination: Principles and procedures of creative thinking.* New York: Charles Scribner's Sons.

Paul, R., & Elder, L. (2001). *Critical thinking: Tools for taking charge of your learning and your life.* Upper Saddle River, NJ: Prentice Hall.

Paul, R., Biner, A. J. A., Jensen, K., & Kreklau, H. (1987). A guide for remodeling lesson plans in language arts and social studies and science. *Critical Thinking Handbook: 4th–6th Grades.* Rohnert Park, CA: Center for Critical Thinking and Moral Critique, Sonoma State University.

Payne, R. K. (2001). *A framework for understanding poverty.* Highlands, TX: aha! Process, Inc.

Paulk, W. (1984). *How to study in colldge,* 3rd ed. Boston: Houghton Mifflin.

Pear, J. "Teaching and Researching High Order Thinking in a Virtual Environment," Retrieved May 31, 2004, from http://home.cc.umanitoba.ca/~capsi/ capsipapers2.htm

Perkins, D., & Blythe, T. (1994, February). Putting understanding up front. *Educational Leadership, 59,* (5), 4–7.

Phelan, P, (Ed.). (1996). *High interest-easy reading: An annotated book list for middle school and senior high school.* Urbana, IL: National Council for Teachers of English.

Picture Books for Older Readers. Retrieved May 20, 2003, from http://www.srv.net /~gale/older.html

Problem Solving Types in Education and Career Development. Retrieved May 29, 2004; available from http://info-center.ccit.arizona.edu/~discover/problem_solving.htm

Raiteri, S. Recommended graphic novels for public libraries. Retrieved May 8, 2004, from http://www.my.voyager.net/~raiteri/graphicnovels.htm

REAP Central. Retrieved May 31, 2004, from http://members.aol.com/ReadShop /REAP1.htm

Reis, S. M., Kaplan, S. N., Tomlinson, C. A., Westberg, K. L., Callahan, C. M., & Cooper, C. R. (1998 November). A response: Equal does not mean identical. *Educational Leadership, 56,* (3), 74–77.

Renzulli, J. S. (1977). *The enrichment triad model,* Mansfield Center, CT: Creative Learning Press.

Richardson, W. (2003, September). Web logs in the english classroom: More than just a chat. *English Journal, 93,* (1), 39–43.

Richison, J. D., Hernandex, A. C., & Carter, M. (2002, November). Blending multiple genre in theme baskets. *The English Journal,* 76–81.

Rogalle, M. Future problem solving program. Retrieved May 29, 2004, from http://www. gifted.uconn.edu/nrcgt/newsletter/spring03/spring032.htm

Rubenzer, R. (2003). *How to best handle stress.* Warren Publishing.

Santa, C., & Havens, I. (1991). Learning through writing. In C. Santa, & D. Alvermann (Eds.), *Science learning: Processes and applications.* Newark, DE: International Reading Association.

Scenario Writing Component Alabama Future Problem Solving Program. Retrieved May 29, 2004, from http://webpages.charter.net/fpsofalabama/scenario.htm

Schiever, S. W. (1971). *A comprehensive approach to teaching thinking.* Boston: Allyn and Bacon.

Schwartz, R. M. (1988). Learning to learn vocabulary in content area textbooks, *Journal of Reading,* 113.

Science voyages: Grade 6. (2000). Columbus, OH: Glencoe/McGraw Hill, 414–421.

Senge, Peter. 2000. *Schools that learn.* New York: First Currency (Doubleday).

Siegle, D. (2000, September). Interesting and Entertaining Internet sites for Kids. *Teaching for High Potential, II,* (2), 3–4.

Silver, H. F., Strong, R. W., & Perini, M. J. (2000). *So each may learn: Integrating learning styles and multiple intelligences.* Alexandria, VA: Association for Curriculum and Supervision Development.

Soloman, & Felder. (1993). The index of learning styles questionnaire. Retrieved May 17, 2004, from http://www.engr.ncsu.edu/learningstyles/ilsweb.htm

Stepien, W. J, & Pyke, S. L. (1997 Summer). Designing problem-based learning units. *Journal for the Education of the Gifted, 20,* (4), 380–400.

Sullivan, D. (Ed.). Search engine watch. Retrieved October 25, 2003, from www.search enginewatch.com

Systematic inventive thinking innovation. Retrieved June 3, 2004, from www.sitsite.com

Taba, H. (1962). *Curriculum development, theory and practice.* New York: Harcourt Brace & World.

Taba, H. (1967). *Teachers handbook for elementary social students (intro ed).* Palo Alto, CA: Addison-Wesley.

Tarquin, P., & Walker, S. (1997). *Creating success in the classroom: Visual organizers and how to use them.* Englewood, CO: Teacher Ideas Press.

The 4Mat system by Bernice McCarthy. Retrieved May 17, 2004, from http://www.about learning.com

The Myers-Briggs Type Indicator (Jung Test). Retrieved September 13, 2004, from http://www.humanmetrics.com

The six-step problem solving model. Retrieved May 29, 2004, from www.paly.nct/~dbertain/eng-ed/Robotics/robo/guide/prob-solv.html.

The learner's dimension (Kathleen Butler's homepage). Retrieved June 3, 2004, from http://www.learnersdimension.com

Tinkertoys and Michael Michalko. Retrieved June 1, 2004, from www.thelearning web.net/chapter05/page198.html

Tomlinson, C. A. (1993, September). Independent study: A flexible tool for encouraging academic and personal growth. *Middle School Journal, 25,* 55–59.

Tomlinson, C. (1995). *How to differentiate instruction in the mixed ability classroom.* Alexandria, VA: Association for Supervision and Curriculum Development.

Tomlinson, C. A. & Kalbfleisch, M. L. (1998, November). Teach me, teach my brain: A call for differentiated classrooms. *Educational Leadership, 56,* (3), 52–55.

Tomlinson, C., & Imbeau, M. (1999, April). A focus on independent study. *Teaching for High Potential, 1,* (1), 1–4.

Tomlinson, C. A. (2000, April). Complex instruction: A powerful cooperative strategy. *Teaching For High Potential, II,* (1), 1–4.

Tomlinson, C. A., Kaplan, S., Renzulli, J., Purcell, J., Lappien, J., Burns, D. E. (2001). The parallel curriculum. Thousand Oak, CA: Corwin Press.

Thomason, T., & York, C. (2000). *Write on target: Preparing Young writers to succeed on state writing achievement tests.* Norwood, MA: Christopher-Gordan Publishers. Inc.

Traver, R. (1998, March). What is a good guiding question? *Educational Leadership, 55,* (6), 70–73.

Tucker, B., Hafenstein, N. L., Jones, S., Bernick, R., & Haines, K. (1997, June). An integrated-thematic curriculum for gifted learners. *Roper Review, 19,* (4), 196–199.

Unit 5: East Asia and South East Asia. (1998). *Africa, Asia and Pacific realm.* Raleigh, NC: NC State University.

Weblogs at Harvard Law. (2003). What makes a weblog a weblog? Retrieved October 25, 2003, from http://blogs.law.harvard.edu/waht

Weiderhold, C. (1997). *The q-matrix/cooperative learning and higher-level thinking.* San Clemente, CA: Kagan Cooperative Learning.

Welcome to the temperament sorter II: Personality instrument. Retrieved 29 May 2004; available from http://www.advisorteam.com/termperament_sorter/register.asp?partid=1

Willis, S. (1994, October). The well-rounded classroom: Applying the theory of the multiple intelligences. *Update* (ASCD Publication), *36,* (8), 1, 5–9.

Who Invented Moo? (2003). Retrieved October 25, 2003, from http://www.moo.mud.org/moo-faq-1.html

What is a MUD? (2003). Retrieved October 25, 2003, from http://www.mudconnect.com/mudfaq/mudfaq-p1.html

Wiggins, G., & McTighe, J. (1998). *Understanding by design.* Alexandria, VA: Association for Supervision and Curriculum Development.

Wilhelm, J. D. (1997). *You gotta be the book.* Urbana, IL: National Council for Teachers of English.

Winebrenner, S. (1992). *Teaching gifted kids in the regular classroom.* Minneapolis, MN: Free Spirit Publishing, Inc

Wolf, D. P. (1988). *Reading reconsidered: Literature and literacy in high school.* New York: The College Board.

Wood, K. D. (1983). A variation on an old theme: Four way oral reading. *The Reading Teacher, 37,* 38–41.

Wood, K. D. (1994). *Practical strategies for improving instruction.* Columbus, Ohio: National Middle School Association.

Wood, K. (2001). *Strategies for integrating reading and writing.* Winterville, OH: National Middle School Association.

World cultures and geography: Western hemisphere and Europe. (2003). Evanston, IL: McDougal Littell.

X, M., From *The autobiography of Malcolm X in 1994: Literature and language (red level).* Evanston, IL: McDougal Littell.

Yancey, K. B. (Ed.). (1992). *Portfolios in the writing classroom: An introduction.* Urbana, IL: National Council of Teachers of English.

Zemelman, S., Daniels, H., & Hyde, A. (1998). *Best practice: New standards for teaching and learning in America's schools,* 2d ed. Portsmouth, NH: Heineman.